Carl Dolmetsch:
A Centenary Celebration

A musical miscellany compiled and edited by
Jeanne Dolmetsch & Andrew Mayes

Carl Dolmetsch: **A Centenary Celebration**

© Andrew Mayes and Jeanne Dolmetsch 2011

Published in the United Kingdom by
Peacock Press,
Scout Bottom Farm,
Mytholmroyd,
West Yorkshire HX7 5JS
Tel: 01422 882751
Fax: 01422 886157

ISBN 978-1-904846-72-7

Design and artwork, D&P Design and Print
Printed by Lightning Source (UK)

Carl Dolmetsch:
A Centenary Celebration

A musical miscellany compiled and edited by
Jeanne Dolmetsch & Andrew Mayes

Peacock Press

There is a performing score with recorder parts available free of charge to purchasers of this volume. It may be requested by email - jerry@recordermail.co.uk
or by post to Recorder Music*Mail*, Scout Bottom Farm, Mytholmroyd, Hebden Bridge HX7 5JS (UK)

CONTENTS

Introduction 1

Carl Dolmetsch – A Tribute by Edgar Hunt 3

Carl Dolmetsch – the Recorder Maker 9

Carl Dolmetsch on the Recorder – his writings and articles 15

The Wigmore Hall Recitals 1939-1989 23

A Wealth of Important Correspondence 41

Works composed for Carl Dolmetsch and Joseph Saxby 47

Birthday Pieces Composed for Carl Dolmetsch 61

A Gavotte for Four Recorders 67

Two Pieces for Bass Recorder and Harpsichord 69

Pieces for Two Recorders (ONE player) 75

Studies to Improve Recorder Technique 81

ACKNOWLEDGEMENTS

We are very grateful to the following people for their kind permission to publish material in this Centenary Celebration Album:

Erica and David Bendix, for the inclusion of Walter Bergmann's *Fuga à 3*.

Greta Dolmetsch, for the inclusion of 'Echoes from the past - a Brandenburg broadcast'.

William Godfree, for the inclusion of *C. F. D. – A Birthday Present*, for descant recorder and piano.

Margaret Hyatt-Jacob, for the inclusion of Gordon Jacob's *Unfinished 70-note Tune for Carl's ...ieth Birthday*, facsimile of Postcard from Gordon Jacob to Carl Dolmetsch dated 21st May 1957, and extracts of other letters from Gordon Jacob to Carl Dolmetsch.

Joan Johnson, for the inclusion of Reginald Johnson's *Sonatina Domestica* for descant recorder and harpsichord.

Rosemary Marciniak, for the inclusion of the facsimile of the obituary for Carl Dolmetsch by Edgar Hunt.

Michael Short, for the inclusion of *Giocata* for descant recorder and harpsichord, and *Les Quatre Vingts – fantaisie sur le nom 'C. D.'* for descant recorder solo

The Trustees of the estate of Edwin York Bowen, for the inclusion of the facsimiles of Bowen's programme note for his *Sonatina* op. 121 for recorder and piano.

Adrian Yardley, for the inclusion of facsimiles of letters from Edmund Rubbra to Carl Dolmetsch dated 12th March 1949 and 10th September 1964, and extracts of other letters from Edmund Rubbra to Carl Dolmetsch.

INTRODUCTION

It is a happy fact that within the world of music significant anniversaries are frequently marked in any number of ways; concerts, recitals, new pieces, lectures, publications, conferences and all sorts of other events organised to celebrate the lives of musicians and their work.

2011 is the centenary of the birth of Carl Dolmetsch, surely one of the most influential figures of the recorder's extraordinary revival in the 20th century. From the moment when, as a seven-year-old boy, he accidentally left the bag containing his father's precious Bressan treble recorder on a platform at Waterloo Station, his life was inextricably bound up with an instrument cherished throughout the earlier periods of its long history. His subsequent work as a player, maker, writer, teacher and, above all, dedicated champion of the instrument demands to be celebrated in a tangible and practical way.

The Dolmetsch archive at 'Jesses', the Dolmetsch family home in Haslemere, contains a wealth of material in the form of manuscripts, correspondence, recital programmes, press cuttings and photographs. We have collected together various items from this unique collection (and other sources), most of them previously unpublished, to present a portrait of the man and his music making. Among the musical manuscripts are those of works by Carl himself and of a number of composers who wrote new pieces for him, and in some instances his musical colleague of some 60 years, the harpsichordist Joseph Saxby (whose centenary it was in 2010). It has been possible to reproduce all or part of the selected musical manuscripts in facsimile. However, we felt it was essential for this music to be included in a form in which it could be easily and conveniently played, so all the chosen items have also been computer set in score and, where required, with separate recorder parts.

Amongst the other material we have included are facsimiles of just a few of the fascinating letters from composers. Carl's encouragement of some of the most distinguished composers of the 20th century to write new works for the recorder is perhaps his most important and far-reaching contribution to the instrument's modern revival. These first performances became an eagerly awaited element of his annual Wigmore Hall recitals given over a period of 50 years. The programmes of the first two and last of these recitals have been included in facsimile. From these it will be seen that, in addition to the modern works, the repertoire of the recorder's past also occupied an important place. But we must not overlook the other aspects of his work, especially that of recorder maker, in which his inventiveness led to the introduction of the bell key and lip key, two devices, the fundamentals of which have continued to be explored by succeeding generations of recorder makers.

Both Carl and Joseph toured extensively, particularly to the USA and Canada, but also to Australia, New Zealand, Japan, South America and almost the whole of Europe. Yet they gave innumerable recitals in the UK, not only in some of the most important concert venues, but also to schools – Carl appreciated that children were the recorder players of the future and spent considerable time introducing them to the instrument, an activity in which he revealed a natural ability for communicating with young people, earning himself the title of 'Pied Piper of Haslemere!'

We hope you will enjoy this Celebratory Album as much as we have enjoyed assembling it. In addition to the music presented for you to play, something Carl would have welcomed and encouraged, there is an abundance of other material of considerable interest to a recorder world to which he contributed so much and for which it remains grateful in this his centenary year and, indeed, will continue to be so in the years to come.

Jeanne Dolmetsch and Andrew Mayes
November 2010

Carl Dolmetsch: **A Centenary Celebration**

Carl demonstrating the recorder to a group of school children with Joseph at the harpsichord

CARL DOLMETSCH – A TRIBUTE BY EDGAR HUNT

Andrew Mayes recalls: when Carl Dolmetsch died in July 1997 I was the editor of *The Recorder Magazine* at the time, and was determined that space would be devoted to appropriate tributes and, particularly, a comprehensive obituary. I could think of nobody more qualified to write this than Edgar Hunt. Edgar had been a co-founder with Carl of the Society of Recorder Players in 1937; indeed they were the society's first musical directors. They both took part in the seminal recital at a studio meeting of the London Contemporary Music Centre in June 1939 in which newly composed works for recorder and keyboard by Lennox Berkeley, Stanley Bate, Peter Pope and Christian Darnton received their first performances. Edgar played baroque flute in a number of recitals at the Haslemere Festival and also took part as a recorder player in at least one of Carl's Wigmore Hall recitals in the late 1940s. A long-time member of the Dolmetsch Foundation, Edgar attended meetings well into the later years of his life, usually insisting on walking from Haslemere railway station to 'Jesses' – a considerable distance.

A veritable mine of information on the recorder, Edgar had an astonishing memory for detail. When, in 1998, I asked him about the London Contemporary Music Centre recital given in June 1939, and particularly the new work by Christian Darnton, which the composer had withdrawn, Edgar recalled it as if it had taken place only months rather than almost sixty years previously. Apparently, though there was nothing intrinsically wrong with the piece musically, the writing was rather unidiomatic for the recorder, making frequent use of double tonguing in its lowest register and perhaps more suited to the clarinet.

Edgar was also renowned for his elegant handwriting, and rarely if ever resorted to a typewriter, certainly for correspondence. So when I asked him if he would write an obituary for Carl he willingly accepted, apologising that it would be hand written. However, I firmly assured him that this would be entirely satisfactory. It duly turned up; a typically detailed and worthy tribute from one important figure in the recorder's 20th-century revival to another. I have retained it as one of those unique documents that will always remain special. In the letter with which Edgar enclosed the obituary he noted, 'I have now acquired a typewriter but I've got to learn how it works – it seems more like a computer!' In a way it was fortuitous that he had not yet mastered the workings of his new typewriter, and the text in his very characteristic hand is reproduced here exactly as it was received.

Carl Frederic Dolmetsch
CBE Dr (Honoris causa, Exeter) Hon. F.T.C.L.
1911 - 1997

Carl, the youngest of the four children of Arnold and Mabel Dolmetsch, devoted his life to music and the recorder. From his father Carl learnt to play the violin and the treble viol, and he grew up in an atmosphere where harpsichords and viols were normal, not 'quaint'. Having lost a treasured Bressan recorder at Waterloo Station in 1919, it was his destiny to lead the revival of that instrument in the 20th century.

In 1919 he was already part of the family's ensemble giving lecture-recitals of what we now call 'Early Music', leading to the First of the Haslemere Festivals in 1925 where the treble recorders were presented in the F major harpsichord concerto of Bach. On this occasion the recorders were played by Carl's older brother Rudolph and Miles Tomalin. The following year the whole consort of descant, treble, tenor and bass recorders made their debut led by Carl's descant.

About 1930 Arnold Dolmetsch was dividing the three main sections of the workshops among his children and their husbands. Cécile and Leslie Ward were in charge of harpsichords, Nathalie and George Carley were responsible for Viols and Violins while Carl was in sole command of Recorders.

Not only did he make descant, treble, tenor and bass tuned to A=415, the pitch adopted by Arnold Dolmetsch for all his concerts from the 1890s, but A=439 (New Philharmonic) which was becoming normal in UK (Military bands had been almost a semitone higher). But Carl had made alto recorders in E flat for Bach's Cantata 106, and an alto in D (voice flute) so that he could play some traverso parts. I had been invited to play traverso in Bach's Peasants' Cantata in 1931. My 'fee' on that occasion was one of the first Dolmetsch sopranino recorders. I was asked to play traverso in pieces where there was a need to contrast the tone qualities of traverso and flauto as in the Quantz Trio Sonata but it was expedient for Carl to play traverso parts on the voice flute. Then, later, Carl revived the sixth flute (descant in D) for Concertos by Woodcock and others.

All this was no mean achievement. Carl could not go to College in London to learn Recorder Making. There were no books on the subject. Nor could he travel to see the instruments in the museums of Europe. He would see a few antique instruments which came to Haslemere for repair. He was not in touch with other makers with whom he could compare notes.

About 1930 Arnold Dolmetsch was responsible for the early Instrumental Music section of the Columbia History of Music: consorts of viols, music for lute and harpsichord etc. On DB 1115 Carl played the Handel F major sonata for recorder with his brother Rudolph (harpsichord) and Rudolph's wife Millicent (viola da gamba), and on DB 1062 he played Greensleeves to a Ground on descant recorder with Nathalie (treble recorder) and Arnold Dolmetsch (Virginals).

In 1932 Carl began his partnership with Joseph Saxby (harpsichord and piano) which took them on concert tours to Australia, New Zealand, U.S.A., Canada and Japan — a partnership which lasted some 50 years (Joseph Saxby died 23 June 1997).

In 1936 I joined the staff of Schott & Co to promote recorder music, much of which was being produced in Germany. I had formed a recorder trio with Max Champion (treble) his wife Stephanie (tenor) and myself (bass). We thought it would be a good idea to form a recorder society so that players who were scattered about the country could be in touch with each other. The Champions heard that Carl was planning something similar: so we all got together and started the SRP in 1937. Max was Chairman; Stephanie, secretary, while Carl and I became joint musical directors. Arnold Dolmetsch was our President until his death in 1940.

In 1937 Carl married Mary Ferguson from Dumfries (Scotland). They had four children: François who now lives in Columbia, twins Jeanne and Marguerite and Richard, a brilliant young musician who died tragically.

Carl was always forward looking and seeking ways to improve the recorder and give in a contemporary rôle: hence the F# key, the echo key and the tone projector. On 1 February 1939 he gave his first full-length recital at London's Wigmore Hall with Joseph Saxby at the harpsichord. In the absence of any 20th century solos he composed his own Theme and Variations to show what the recorder could do. This was the first of his annual 'Wigmores', a series which continued for 45 years. The report of the concert in The Recorder News No 2 (1938-40) was written by "Terpander" = Manuel Jacobs, an enthusiastic young recorder player who also wanted a 'modern' repertoire for the recorder and had been encouraging his friends among composers to write Sonatinas for recorder and piano. These were not in time for Carl's first Wigmore; but Carl and I played four of them at a meeting of the London Contemporary Music Centre on 17 June 1939. The two which Carl played were by Stanley Bate and Lennox Berkeley, and he included the Berkeley in his second Wigmore which was on 18 November 1939. Most of these works were published by Schott.

During the War the Dolmetsch workshops turned over to making aircraft components, and there were no more recorders for the duration. Dolmetsch recorders were the best hand-made recorders, and could not be produced in large numbers. I had been supplying the 'Lower end of the market' through Schott with imports from Germany. But stocks in this country were exhausted before Christmas 1939, while the demand was increasing, mainly from schools which had been evacuated to the country, with no pianos to lead the singing. To fill this gap I designed an 'economy' recorder for Schott which could be made in plastic and sell for 4/6 (about 23p). Carl was against this at first but soon realized that any child with one of these instruments was a potential customer for one of his after the war.

I fact, after the War, excellent plastic recorders were produced to Carl's design while the hand-made ones continued and are now in the hands of Jeanne and Marguerite with the addition of son in law Dr Brian Blood.

The end of the War saw the revival of the SRP and the addition of Walter Bergmann and Freda Dinn to the Society's Musical Directors. The four of us worked together to found the Recorder in Education Summer School, originally at Roehampton, but gradually moving further North, while Carl started the Dolmetsch Summer School nearer to Haslemere.

Carl was always faithful to his father's teachings; but he continued to seek a place for the recorder in the present, and, as his Wigmore recitals continued he commissioned new works from leading composers, including

Some with string quartet and other instruments. Among the composers who contributed to this repertoire were Herbert Murrill, Cyril Scott, York Bowen, Hans Gal, Arnold Cooke, Gordon Jacob, Edmund Rubbra and many more.

Arnold Dolmetsch died in February 1940, but Carl had already, in 1937, been given responsibility for the Festival, kept it going during the War years (in reduced form), and celebrated the Silver Jubilee in 1950 and the 40th in 1964. He also adopted British Standard Pitch for the Festivals and his own recitals to encourage cooperation with artists, particularly singers and string quartets from the outside world of music.

Carl's love of nature and in particular the gay plumage of birds — he kept pheasants at one time — spread to his music where he was identified with Le rossignol en amour (Couperin), The Goldfinch (Cosyn), Woody Cock (Farnaby) and Robin (Mundy). He enjoyed his concert tours with Joseph Saxby and made many friends. He was a success with children and was the Pied Piper of Haslemere to them.

Carl was born in France at Fontenay sur Bois near Paris where his father was making harpsichords for Gaveau; but the family returned to London soon afterwards, settling eventually at Haslemere in Surrey. French was the language spoken in the family, and Carl never lost the french accent of his youth. His marriage to Marie did not last. A few weeks before he died he married Greta Matthews who had been his secretary and 'one of the family' for close on 60 years.

Edgar Hunt

Carl Frederic Dolmetsch CBE Dr.(Honoris causa, Exeter) Hon. F.T.C.L.

23rd August 1911 – 11th July 1997

CARL DOLMETSCH – THE RECORDER MAKER

Carl received his early instrumental tuition from his father Arnold, and was just seven years old when he made his debut with the family consort playing the viol. He later also learned the violin, but it was to be some years before he was introduced to the recorder, and then in rather extraordinary circumstances. The recorder had featured as a solo instrument in the first Haslemere Festival in 1925, with a performance of Bach's F major harpsichord concerto, in which the recorders were played by Carl's older brother Rudolph and Miles Tomalin. At the following year's Festival Bach's fourth Brandenburg Concerto was to be performed, but circumstances led to Carl, who had not previously played the recorder, being 'thrown in at the deep end', as Greta Dolmetsch described in the programme of the 76th Haslemere Festival in 2000:

ECHOES FROM THE PAST – A BRANDENBURG BROADCAST

As the now familiar and well-loved strains of Bach's fourth Brandenburg Concerto resound through the Haslemere Hall at the conclusion of this year's Saturday afternoon concert, it is interesting to reflect on an earlier occasion seventy-four years ago, when this work was the opening item in the second Haslemere Festival.

On Tuesday 24th August 1926 musical history was made, as for the first time since the 18th century, Bach's fourth Brandenburg Concerto was performed with recorders, two treble recorders in G or "flauti d'echo", which Arnold Dolmetsch had successfully recreated earlier that year. The two recorder parts were played by Arnold's sons, Rudolph and Carl, and for Carl this was a particularly auspicious occasion as it was his unexpected début on the recorder. The second part was originally to have been played by the young Cambridge graduate Miles Tomalin, but just weeks before the concert his father, (the managing director of Jaegers and future chairman of the Dolmetsch Foundation) insisted that his son accompany the family on a holiday to Switzerland. Emergency measures had to be taken and Arnold turned to his son Carl and said, "you will do it".

So in just five weeks Carl, assisted by his elder brother Rudolph, mastered the part and on the day following his fifteenth birthday found himself on the Haslemere Hall stage, not in his accustomed role as violinist but as a recorder soloist, standing next to his brother and his father who was playing the solo violin part, and surrounded by an orchestra composed of his friends and family.

But this was not all, for the performance was to be broadcast 'live' by the British Broadcasting Company, as it was then known, by means of a landline from Haslemere to Daventry. It had been intended to relay only the first half of the concert, but, such was the audience's enthusiasm for the music, that one of the engineers stationed backstage hurried to the public telephone in the post office to persuade headquarters at 2LO to transmit the second half of the concert and delay the scheduled programme of the Savoy Orpheans. Carl Dolmetsch never forgot the electrifying atmosphere in the hall that night, the thrill of being allowed to listen to the music through headphones for the first time and of hearing the excited voice of the chief engineer saying to the bosses "You can't stop this now...you must let it go on".

And thus it was that Brandenburg IV and the entire opening concert of the second Haslemere Festival was broadcast live to the outside world while the Orpheans had to wait – those were the days!

GRETA DOLMETSCH

Carl Dolmetsch: **A Centenary Celebration**

Having learned to turn on the Dolmetsch workshop lathes, and also now possessing the technique to play the recorder, Carl was taught by his father to voice and tune the instrument. His acquisition of the necessary skills was rapid, and while still in his teens, he was entrusted with the entire programme of design, manufacture and promotion of Dolmetsch recorders. Although he continued to play the viol and violin (and did so for the rest of his life), from this time on Carl's preoccupation with the recorder was to take on far greater significance.

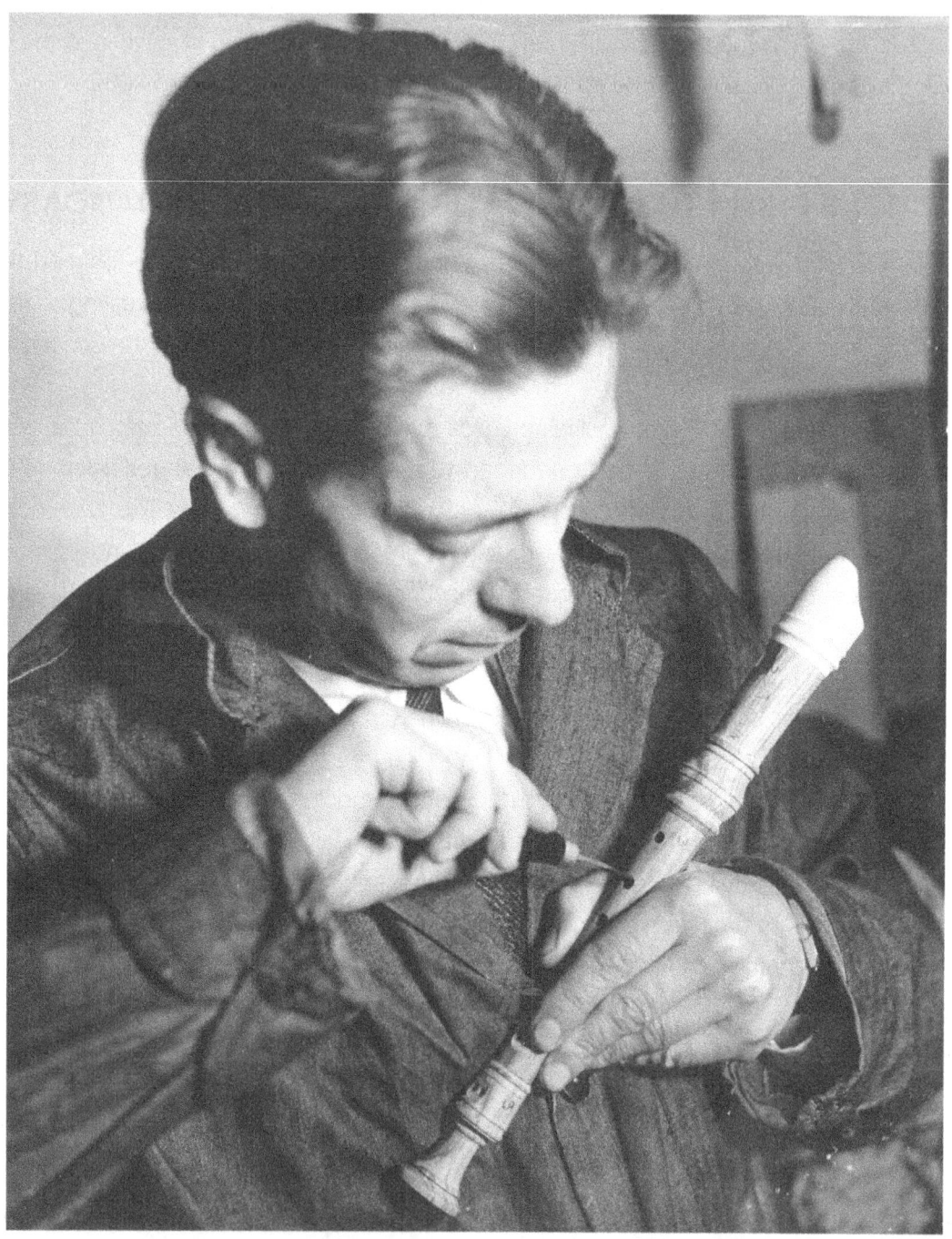

Carl Dolmetsch undercutting a finger hole on a descant recorder

Arnold Dolmetsch was renowned as an innovator who constantly sought ways to advance the manufacture and function of the musical instruments he made. Carl also inherited this inquisitiveness and brought the same inventiveness to the recorder. He took a very pragmatic approach and didn't feel restricted to copying historic instruments exactly, noting in an interview, 'I am not personally interested in an instrument that can't also meet the demands of the modern composer'. A number of innovative solutions were, as a result, introduced to overcome some of the technical problems experienced with old recorders.

One of these was the missing high F# on the treble instrument. Some early fingering charts ventured a solution, but significantly Hotteterre's recorder fingering chart in his *Principles of the Flute, Recorder and Oboe* published in 1707 doesn't include the note. Carl had developed a method of playing high F#, but this made use of what he sometimes referred to as a 'trick' fingering and involved slurring up from the E or F immediately below; it would not sound if not slurred. However, the principles for a more practical method were discovered by accident, as Carl recalled;

> In 1929, when I happened to be practising while seated, I discovered to my astonishment and delight that by stopping the end of my treble recorder with my knee, and fingering as for high F natural or top G, I could produce a firm pure and reliable high F sharp.

This led to the idea of a mechanical solution:

> My immediate intention was to fit a key to the end-piece, to be operated by the right-hand little finger. The stress of meeting the enormous demand for standard models temporarily deflected me from my good intentions and I continued to employ my trick fingerings.

It was indeed to be some years before the key came into use, as Carl explained:

> Although the bell key had existed in my mind for so long, it was not until 1957, (the year Gordon Jacob wrote his Suite for me) that I actually put my invention into effect, and used it at my Wigmore Hall recital on 31st January 1958.

He eventually patented his invention in 1958 (Patent number GB 852165). Initially, this indicated the hole at the foot of the bore of the instrument plugged, and an alternative hole positioned on the side of the instrument close to the bottom end of the foot. This hole was covered by an open key to be operated by the little finger of the right hand, as shown in the drawing that accompanied the patent application reproduced below.

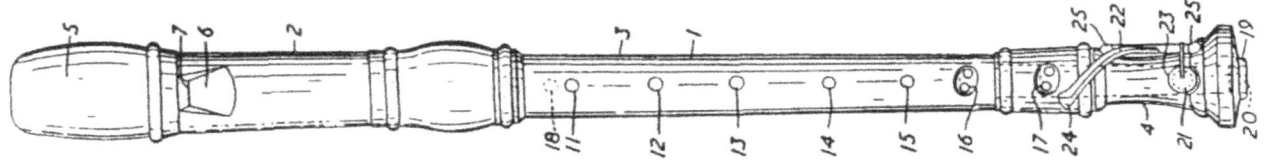

Drawing that accompanied the original patent application for the bell key

The specification with the patent application explained that there were constructional problems in providing a key to cover the hole at the foot of the bell in its traditional location. However, these problems were eventually overcome, and the device finally introduced included an elegant key covering the hole in the foot of the bell in its traditional position, as shown in the photographs below.

A bell key fitted to the foot joint of a Dolmetsch treble recorder, instrument No. 10740

(Photograph by Alison Mayes)

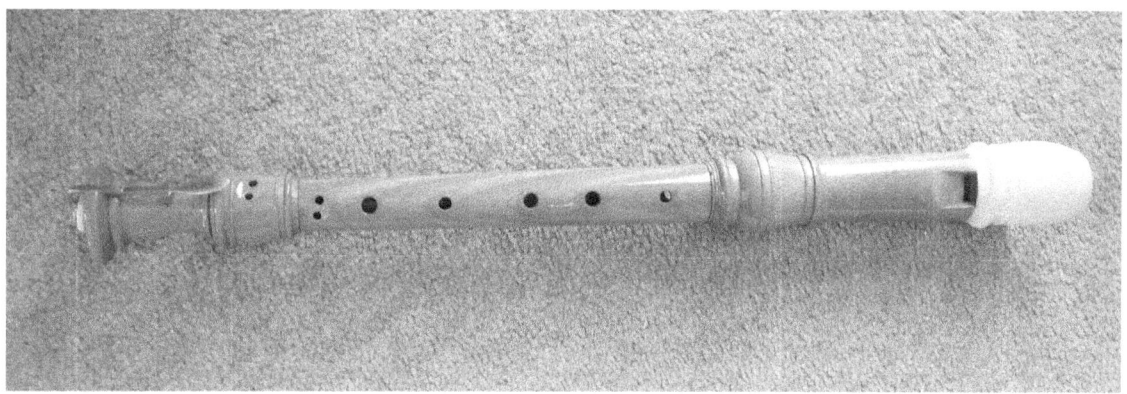

Dolmetsch treble recorder, instrument No. 10740

(Photograph by Alison Mayes)

The bell key not only enabled the high F# to be obtained, but also the top A and B-flat above that, thus completing the treble recorder's chromatic compass right up to top c (the note present in the last movement of Telemann's F major recorder sonata) and was later added to smaller sizes of recorder where it served the same function. Carl also made use of it in some alternative soft and loud fingerings, and these are sometimes indicated in his annotated performing material.

Use of the bell key to obtain these high notes is explained in volume three of Carl's recorder tutor, *Advanced Recorder Technique* in which he also described another totally different function:

> Further still, the use of the key can produce a timbre somewhat resembling clarinet quality, though as this slightly lowers the pitch of certain notes within the operative compass, care must be taken to regulate the intonation by judicious control of breath pressure. The range over which the "clarinet" effect can be used is from low A to G, (omitting the little finger from its twin holes for playing B-flat) on the treble (alto), and from low E to D on the descant (soprano).

Though not as frequently employed, Carl's annotations that may indicate its use are present in the fifth movement of the manuscript of Alan Ridout's *Sequence* for recorder and lute from which the first performance was given at the Wigmore Hall in 1975.

The recorder is frequently perceived as having a severely limited dynamic range, at least when compared with other wind instruments. This too exercised Carl's mind and in the 1930s he experimented with various devices that reduced the volume of air impinging on the labium edge to produce a quieter note. However, he eventually abandoned this in favour of a device working in an entirely different way, and the lip (or echo) key was patented in 1958 (Patent number GB 852135). The lip key works on the principle that a small hole drilled into the bore, near the line of the block, slightly raises the pitch of the entire instrument (a principle well-known to bamboo pipe makers who form three very small-diameter holes near the block line to fine tune their instruments).

Carl's key covered one small hole drilled just below the block line. This is indicated by the numbers 21, 22 and 23 on the drawing below (that accompanied the patent application). With the key closed the instrument remains at its normal pitch, but with the key open the pitch is slightly raised. To restore the pitch, breath pressure is lowered, and the volume is therefore reduced. Though Carl might have arranged for the key to be operated by the little finger of the left hand (the one finger that is not used to cover a finger hole), he chose instead for it to be lowered against the chin while retaining the mouthpiece between the lips. He therefore had the facility to play a genuinely softer note while maintaining control over intonation.

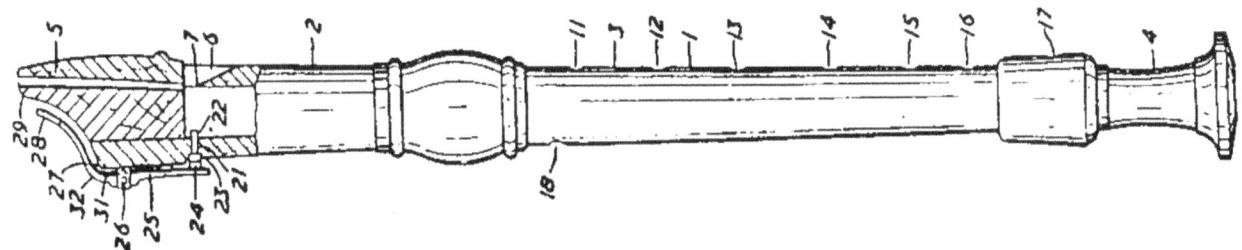

Drawing that accompanied the patent application for the lip key

There are places in the performing material for some of the contemporary works composed for Carl (notably Gordon Jacob's *Suite* and *Variations*, and Arthur Milner's *Suite*) where a specific sign has been annotated which can be interpreted only as indicating use of the lip key. This is confirmed in the case of Jacob's *Variations* in the recording of the work Carl made with Joseph Saxby in 1974 in which the effect of the lip key is clearly audible.

Another device that Carl introduced, though not actually forming a permanent part of the instrument, was the tone projector. He discovered that by placing his fingers, 'slightly curled alongside the window, the volume of tone was at once greater', and further explained:

> This led to the production of a small four-sided "cowl", somewhat resembling a bottomless wheelbarrow! …The tone projector (Brit. Pat No 666602) is designed to enhance, but in no way distort the natural tone colour of the recorder.

The device was made particular use of when performing with larger ensembles of modern instruments and in larger concert venues.

Though the bell key has not been as universally adopted as its usefulness might suggest a number of players do make use of it, particularly in 20th-century repertoire, and some recorders are now being made with extended foot joints and key work that do permit the high F# to be obtained with straightforward fingerings.

Versions of the lip key have continued to be introduced on recorders of modern design, and the innovative harmonic tenor recorder developed and made by Maarten Helder has an 'echo' key working on exactly the same principle as the Dolmetsch lip key, though operated by the little finger of the left hand. More like the lip key is the chin-operated slide mechanism to control dynamics fitted to some Ganassi-type recorders by the Dutch maker Adriana Breukink. The discoveries made by Carl Dolmetsch over eighty years ago, and which he developed and introduced as practical additions to the recorder have continued to be developed in various forms by makers today.

CARL DOLMETSCH ON THE RECORDER – HIS WRITINGS AND ARTICLES

Over the years Carl contributed a number of articles on various aspects of the recorder to several musical publications. Among these, those describing the establishment of a contemporary recorder repertoire, especially the new works composed for him, were perhaps the most substantial, but he also covered recorder construction, particularly the various inventions described in the section on Carl Dolmetsch the recorder maker.

His earliest article devoted to the contemporary repertoire, 'An Introduction to the Recorder in Modern British Music', was published in *The Consort*, Volume 17 (1960). This was followed in 1968 by 'The Recorder's 20th Century Repertoire' published in *Recorder and Music Magazine* Volume 2, No. 8, (February 1968). In the Dolmetsch archive is a copy of the article from *The Consort* in which there is a substantial number of annotations in Carl's hand. It is possible that these were made to formulate a draft text for his 1968 article, but in the event, although containing some of the same information, this was written afresh. The earlier article, in which Carl's annotations have as far as practical been incorporated, is reproduced in its entirety below.

AN INTRODUCTION TO THE RECORDER IN MODERN BRITISH MUSIC

BY
CARL DOLMETSCH

THE RENAISSANCE of the recorder (English flute) on a vast scale during the last forty-five years constitutes a phenomenon in the world of music and education. The instrument is more universally played now than at any time during its history and is also the most played of any serious musical instrument, ancient or modern. When Arnold Dolmetsch introduced this English Flute to 20th-century audiences his first objective was to present the instrument's rich repertoire from past centuries. However, it soon became obvious that its tonal and technical resources need by no means be confined to early music alone. Arnold Dolmetsch himself, always the champion of great early music, was also the first in our time to compose for the recorder. In 1928, he wrote a suite on traditional lines for recorder trio.[1] Its three attractive movements consist of a *Fantasie* in the form of a fugue; a contemplative and expressive *Ayre*; and a lively *Jigg* in dotted six-eight rhythm. The next appearance of the of the recorder in modern music in this country is thought to have been in Robin Milford's oratorio *A Prophet in the Land*, composed in 1930.[2]

In the meantime, the interest aroused among German makers and musicians attracted to the Haslemere Festival by Arnold Dolmetsch's activities as early as 1925, resulted in the recorder gaining in popularity in both Germany and Switzerland. This development, which was soon to extend into a world-wide movement, in turn led to the next important work, this time in Germany in 1932. Hindemith's famous Trio was written for a musical meeting at a school in Plön, where the composer himself played it with two friends. This trio in

---
1 Published in 1937 by the Society of Recorder Players and now in Schott's catalogue.
2 Published by O.U.P.

three movements received its first performance in England in June 1939 when, in company with two other members of my family, I presented it at a Studio meeting of the London Contemporary Music Centre. It stood then as an adventurous and, for some time, isolated example of modern recorder writing, so far as the continent was concerned. However, in Britain, the traditional home of the recorder and appropriately the country of its rebirth, events moved much faster.

By the late 1930s the recorder playing population had attained substantial proportions, and a mass of rediscovered early works and arrangements provided an abundance of material to play. Yet the need for a balanced repertoire offering modern as well as early music was fast becoming apparent. This need was voiced by members of the Press, among them Sir Jack Westrup. Reporting from Haslemere for the *Daily Telegraph* on 19th July 1938 he wrote: "These winning instruments are unjustly neglected today. A composer who would write a quartet for them, instead of wringing painful novelty from trumpet or violin, could earn no small gratitude." At this time there was no modern solo music for recorder. It was this conspicuous lack which prompted me later that year to write a theme and variations for descant recorder and harpsichord for my first all-recorder recital at the Wigmore Hall on 1st February 1939. Written in Paganini style, the object was to give a lead to British composers to provide solo music exploiting the instrument's scope for virtuosity, chromatic completeness and tonal variety in a way not afforded by works written before 1800. After this venture, I found a valuable ally in Mr. Manuel Jacobs, whose enthusiasm led him to approach ten composers of the younger British school (as they were then) to ask them to write solo works for the recorder. Four months later, at a studio concert of the London Contemporary Music Centre in June 1939, my colleague Edgar Hunt and I, together with Joseph Saxby at the harpsichord, performed four of these works by Christian Darnton, Peter Pope, Stanley Bate and Lennox Berkeley, whose Sonatina has remained among the most popular ever since.[3] Sir Jack Westrup then reported in the *Daily Telegraph*: "The recorder has hitherto been associated with the revival of music of the 17th and 18th centuries. At the London Contemporary Music Centre's studio meeting on Saturday afternoon we learnt how it could serve the composer of today. The result was encouraging. Provided that an instrument is mechanically perfect – as the modern recorder is – there is clearly no reason why it should be confined to the music of the past ... Not all the composers represented in Saturday's programme had thoroughly grasped either the character of the technique of the instrument. But the concert as a whole proved a serious intention to establish and justify the relationship between the seductive instrument and the music of our time."

The outbreak of war proved a major setback and resulted in delays to the printing of new works and to some being shelved altogether. Nevertheless, some other successful works resulting from Manuel Jacob's initiative did appear in this twilight period, They included a sonatina by Walter Leigh, elegiac in character and one of the best-contrived for the instrument; also a neat and charming little work by Peggy Glanville Hicks. Special mention should be made too of Franz Reizenstein's vigorous and inventive *Partita* op. 13, which I came to know only after the war and have played many times since.[4] Performance of some modern recorder works is affected by the fact that by no means all composers are recorder players, nor do some of them heed the injunctions of players regarding character, technique and in some cases even the compass of the instrument. For instance, a high F-sharp in the third octave of the treble recorder is advisedly best left alone by composers.[5] I well remember my astonishment when one young man, on having this pointed out to him, nonchalantly altered an F-sharp to a natural, making no corresponding amendment to the piano part. He assured me it would make no odds. And he was right!

---

3   Pope's, Bate's and Berkeley's Sonatinas are published by Schott & Co., Ltd.
4   The Leigh and Glanville-Hicks Sonatinas, and Reizenstein's *Partita* are published by Schott & Co., Ltd.
5   By tradition a "missing" note in the otherwise completely chromatic range and therefore accessible only to the highly skilled player.

Despite the difficulties created by war conditions, two works for treble recorder were produced in 1941, one by Anthony Bernard, *Prelude and Scherzo*, and the other by Martin Shaw, his *Sonata in E-flat*, the latter achieving publication during the war.[6] Among earlier works of great charm is a sonatina for descant recorder and piano in one movement by Christopher Edmunds, composed at the suggestion of and dedicated to Edgar Hunt.[7]

With the war over, what had looked like an encouraging beginning to the development of a modern recorder repertoire appeared, by the late 1940s, small and remote. A fresh start had therefore to be made in engaging the interest of leading composers. When I was planning my first post-war recital at Wigmore Hall for the Spring of 1947, Clinton Gray-Fisk (who has shown a considerable interest in modern recorder music) suggested that I approach York Bowen for a work, which was in fact to inaugurate a new series. There resulted his brilliant and substantial Sonata for recorder and piano, in which he played the piano part in the first performance. It is in three movements, the first being in conventional sonata form with two themes and a short section of development. The music moves gently and leans towards the lyrical in style. The second and slower movement remains tranquil in mood and is very free in form. The last movement demands a quick change of recorder from the previous treble to the descant which, like the piccolo, sounds an octave higher than written. Here the music is completely different and shows the more brilliant and agile possibilities of this very effective instrument.

Two years later Edmund Rubbra wrote his noble *Meditazioni sopra 'Cœurs désolés'* op. 67 for recorder and harpsichord.[8] Then, as now, this work made a profound impression, and after the first performance at Wigmore Hall, *The Times* wrote: "... noble music which was nonetheless original and striking for having its roots in the 16th century." The work is constructed on an early French *chanson* and is in one movement divided into sections of varying tempi, the quicker ones being bounded by the main theme at slow tempo supported by rich harmonies in the harpsichord part. This work has had innumerable performances in concerts and broadcasts in many parts of the world.

In 1950, Herbert Murrill wrote a sonata in the four-movement form employed by Handel.[9] Both for the first performance at Wigmore Hall and a subsequent broadcast, the harpsichord part was played by the composer, then Director of Music at the B.B.C. Murrill's love of French music is clearly reflected in this sonata, particularly the first two movements whose invigorating style are at times reminiscent of his piquant *Suite Française* for harpsichord. The third movement is in the form of a contemplative *recitative* and the work concludes with a lively *finale* in gay pastoral vein tinged with an English flavour. Cyril Scott was next to add to the recorder's modern repertoire with his rich and sombre *Aubade*[10] which I played with Joseph Saxby at Wigmore Hall in 1952. This work was valuable both for its musical content and because it proved that 20th-century composers need not be influenced by earlier literature for the recorder, but may write in uninhibited fashion for an instrument whose resources are not restricted to the idioms of the past. In 1953, Antony Hopkins wrote a delightful little suite, dedicated to Walter Bergmann,[11] of which I gave the first performance in Wigmore Hall on 8th May that year. This work, whose movements are *Prelude*, *Scherzo*, *Canon* and *Jig*, made a welcome addition to the fast-growing repertoire, both for its attractive, playful and witty style and because it broke precedent by using the descant instead of the treble recorder, for which most previous works had been designated. A work whose national flavour and originality deserves more

---

6	Published by J. B. Cramer & Co., Ltd.
7	Published by Schott & Co., Ltd.
8	Published by Alfred Lengnick & Co., Ltd.
9	Published by O.U.P.
10	Published by Schott & Co., Ltd.
11	Published by Schott & Co., Ltd.

attention than it has so far received is Norman Fulton's *Scottish Suite* for treble recorder and harpsichord,[12] which received its first performance at Wigmore Hall in 1954. Its movements are *Prelude, Air, Musette, Nocturne* and *Reel*, and its technical demands are well within the scope of the average player.

Although by this time there were appearing more works for recorder with keyboard and for recorder consorts than a recitalist could keep pace with, there was still a conspicuous lack of works for recorder with strings or chamber orchestra in the form so brilliantly exploited by Telemann in his concertos and suites; by Alessandro Scarlatti's sinfonias; and Bach's Brandenburg concertos 2 and 4. Musicians familiar with the rich grandeur of Rubbra's *Meditazioni* eagerly awaited another work from his pen. This time I sought a piece for recorder with string quartet and harpsichord. There resulted a characteristic and beautiful *Fantasia*, op. 86, on a theme by Machaut (c. 1300-1372), which was performed at Wigmore Hall in 1955 with the Martin String Quartet and Joseph Saxby at the harpsichord.[13] Lennox Berkeley followed this with a Concertino for treble recorder with violin, violoncello and harpsichord, op. 48.[14] This was performed at Wigmore Hall in 1956 with Jean Pougnet, Arnold Ashby and Joseph Saxby. The first movement is a slightly modified version of the traditional sonata form. In place of the usual slow movement are two very short pieces entitled *Aria I* and *Aria II*, these are melodic in style and the ensemble is reduced to recorder and 'cello alone for the first Aria, and to violin and harpsichord alone for the second. The last movement is a rondo, considerably lighter in feeling than the others.

Another practice much favoured in the past was that of using the recorder as an obligato instrument – at times on equal terms with the human voice, as in some of the superb cantatas by Bach, Handel and Telemann. When Rubbra offered to write another work, in 1956, I recommended that it should take this form. He responded with *Cantata pastorale* for soprano and recorder, with violoncello and harpsichord, op. 92,[15] which was performed at Wigmore Hall on 1st February, 1957. The cantata was sung by Joan Alexander, with Arnold Ashby, Joseph Saxby and myself. Apart from the difference of scoring, the work was written in a style new for Rubbra. It consisted of linked settings of three poems, the first being by Plato [16] and the second and third are anonymous lyrics from Helen Waddell's *Medieval Latin Lyrics*.[17] All three sections are woven together by transitional material. According to the composer, the pervasive five-note scale E G A-flat B C employed is because its obsessional use in an item of Indian music heard just before the Cantata was begun so impressed itself in the composer's mind that he decided to use it as an appropriate melodic basis for this work.. Having the need for recorder music with string accompaniment ever in mind, I next approached Gordon Jacob – known for his masterly writing for wind instruments – suggesting a work for recorder with string quartet or alternative string orchestra. Dr. Jacob produced a suite of seven movements.[18] The *Prelude, Lament* and *Pavane*, quiet and contemplative in mood, are in contrast to the other four movements which are brisk and rhythmical. The *Burlesca alla Rumba* belongs, as its name suggests, to the category of parody, but it is written affectionately rather than satirically. The *Cadenza* is a kind of improvisatory rumination on the themes of the preceding movements. In the introduction to this movement the 'cello plays an important part. For the final movement, *Tarantella*, the composer recommends the alternative use of the sopranino, which bears the same relationship to the treble recorder as the piccolo does to the flute. The composer has provided an *ad libatum* double bass part to enable the Suite to be played with string orchestra if desired. The first performance in 1958 was given with the Martin String

---

12   Published by Schott & Co., Ltd.
13   Published by Alfred Lengnick & Co., Ltd.
14   Published by J & W Chester/Edition Wilhelm Hansen.
15   Published by Alfred Lengnick & Co., Ltd.
16   Translated by Walter Leaf.
17   One from a Canterbury MS and the other from a Benedictbeuern Monastery MS.
18   Published by O.U.P.

Quartet both at Wigmore Hall and in the subsequent broadcast. It has also been performed orchestrally on a number of occasions, but the scoring is so skilfully devised that the solo recorder is never in danger of being overpowered by the strings.

Robert Simpson, known both as a composer and for his work at the B.B.C., wrote his *Variations and Fugue* for recorder and string quartet in 1959. This work, played at Wigmore Hall on 9th February that year, was also intended as a tribute to his friend and colleague the late Horace Dann. Although serious and even elegiac in parts, it is by no means funereal, and the Fugue is light in texture, swift in pace. The composer follows Gordon Jacob's example of using first treble, then sopranino recorder. At the opening the recorder plays a subsidiary part, the theme being given to violin and viola. Each of the seven variations follows the same trend, and throughout the set there is a gradual increase in tension. The last variation is turbulent and the sopranino recorder is pitted against the strings. After this crisis the music is pulled definitely into the key of E and the Fugue follows, *vivacissimo grazioso*, nearly all *pianissimo* and never rising above *piano*, the sopranino recorder now showing its fleetness and delicacy. At the end the music floats into a slow, gentle, rather sad coda that settles finally in E major. Reference has already been made of the importance of composers making themselves really familiar with the character and technique of the instrument for which they are writing. Arnold Cooke has mastered this principle so thoroughly that he might almost be a clandestine recorder virtuoso. His Concerto for recorder and string orchestra (1957) and *Divertimento* for recorder with string quartet show an uncanny grasp of the recorder's potentialities, which makes his music very rewarding from the player's point of view. The *Divertimento* received its first performance with the Martin String Quartet on 8th February, 1960. The work is mainly light and cheerful, but has a touch of gravity. The first movement reveals its character immediately with a lively melody for the recorder accompanied by a dancing figure in repeated notes on the strings. A subsidiary staccato figure and a second tune for the recorder complete the thematic material, and the movement is in straightforward sonata form. The second movement is more serious in feeling although it is light and simple in texture and construction. It begins with a quiet song-like melody on the recorder. The form is in two parts, the second being a varied repeat of the first. The last movement is a rondo, with the main theme given out by the recorder after four bars' introduction by the quartet. There is also a sprightly second subject which, when it returns in the latter part of the movement, gives the soloist the opportunity to change his instrument to the sopranino.

During the period covered by this survey, recorder works of all kinds have appeared, many of them achieving publication, and of these there is space to cover only a small selection. But mention must be made of works such as Michael Tippett's *Four Inventions* for descant and treble recorders, and Peter Racine Fricker's *Suite* for one tenor and two treble recorders, both commissioned by the Society of Recorder Players. Other works for three recorders include the Suite by Robert Müller-Hartmann, the Suite in G by Timothy Moore, and the *Deddington Suite* by Imogen Holst. Francis Baines has written a Quartet for two treble and two tenor recorders, and a Fantasia for three descant and three treble recorders. Other important works include the *Pastorale* for treble recorder, violin, viola and 'cello by Matyas Seiber,[19] and the Sonatina for treble recorder and piano by Malcolm Arnold.[20] Another most effective work is Benjamin Britten's charming *Alpine Suite* for three recorders.[21] Britten has also made effective use of the recorder in his recent Mystery Play, *Noyes Fludde*.

Peter Crossley-Holland has assembled a vast collection of traditional folk music from many countries, particularly India and China and, nearer home, from Ireland, Wales and Scotland. As a composer, he has the rare gift of combining originality with the marked influence resulting from his intimate knowledge of folk

---
19 All the above-mentioned works are published by Schott & Co., Ltd.
20 Published by Paterson's Publications Ltd.
21 Published by Boosey & Hawkes Ltd.

music. He is also a master of setting ancient and traditional themes within the framework of a modern idiom while still achieving homogeneity. An outstanding example is his five-movement suite *Albion* for three recorders and harpsichord,[22] composed for François, Jeanne, Marguerite and Richard Dolmetsch, who gave the first performance at the Royal Festival Hall Recital Room on 29th April 1959. Each of the five movements was inspired by material from early Scottish MSS. The first, combining unusual rhythmical freedom with a style stemming from medieval organum, is an invocation suggested by fragments of plainchant found in a 13th century MS once at St Andrews. The second is a setting of a piper's tune danced to by some lively witches who were tried in 1659. The melody of the third movement, echoing the music heard by belated travellers in fairy-haunted spots, is re-written from a traditional tune of the Casilles family. The tune of the fourth is partly taken from an air of courtly elegance in a 17th century MS. The playful opening section of the last movement is freely based on some 17th century material having no name. The idea of "The Nameless" suggested the rest of the movement.

The most recent addition to the contemporary consort repertoire has come from Edmund Rubbra, whose *Notturno* for four recorders, op. 106,[23] was written (like Peter Crossley-Holland's *Albion*) for my sons and daughters, who gave the first performance at the Royal Festival Hall Recital Room on 28th April this year. In this piece the composer has exploited the cool sounds of recorder tone by keeping the texture and harmonies bare against the main theme, first stated by the tenor. This substantial three-two theme (in C minor with F-sharp prominent) is treated as a passacaglia. It appears in all four recorder parts, is sometimes inverted, and at one point both the normal and inverted form appear together. There is cumulative movement and, at the final statement of the theme, the descant accompanies it with a dancing theme in four-four, based on a diminution of the cadence bar of the main theme.

[Carl placed a note in the margin here that reads 'Add ref to Hans Gál'. What follows has been introduced by the editors in accordance that intention. Born in Vienna in 1890, Gál had fled to England in 1938 to escape Nazi persecution, and eventually settled in Edinburgh where he became a lecturer in music at Edinburgh University. At the time the original article was published Gál had composed his *Quartettino*, op. 78 for recorder quartet[24] for the Dolmetsch children, but it was not until February 1962 that Carl, together with the Martin String Quartet, gave the first performance of his newly-composed *Concertino* op. 82 for treble recorder and string quartet[25] at the Wigmore Hall. Two further Wigmore Hall premieres followed: his *Trio Serenade*, op. 88, for treble recorder, violin and 'cello,[26] in 1967, and the *Three Intermezzi*, op. 103 for treble recorder and harpsichord (or piano)[27] in 1974. Gál's *Divertimento*, op. 98, for descant, treble and tenor recorders [28] was composed in 1969 for Carl to play with Jeanne and Marguerite.]

The fact that 20th-century composers are writing for the recorder is welcomed by the vast majority of players and adherents. This is not to say that every work from a contemporary pen is automatically a masterpiece. Considerable discrimination is required, but this applies to the music of *any* century and for any instrument. But the fact remains that much music of every era possesses qualities transcending its own time, ensuring survival. No-one at any period should question the rightness of composing new music for an "old" instrument. Had Handel, for instance, taken this view, his recorder sonatas would never have been written. The violin itself is an old instrument, but has been in continuous use, with minor modifications only, since the middle of the 16th century. Composers of each succeeding age have provided it with

---

22   Published by Universal Edition.
23   Published by Alfred Lengnick & Co., Ltd.
24   Published by Universal Edition.
25   Published by Universal Edition.
26   Published by N. Simrock.
27   Published by Schott & Co., Ltd.
28   Published by Schott & Co., Ltd.

"modern" music always different in style from that which had preceded it. The versatility of an instrument and expanding technique of its players have invariably responded to the demands made upon them. This is equally true of the modern recorder, but because this instrument suffered an eclipse for approximately one hundred years of its nine centuries or so of existence, there are still a few people of antiquarian outlook who would confine the recorder to early music and even deny it the right to minor changes in design, voicing or technique intended to increase its ability to meet the needs of both ancient and modern music. We should rejoice that that so many leading composers are writing uninhibited works for the recorder – taking its considerable resources as a matter of course. Any instrument that is to live – and the recorder assuredly is alive all about us – must be given a future as well as a past. This is exactly what contemporary composers are doing today, as did Bach, Handel and Telemann and *their* contemporaries yesterday.

In addition to the two articles mentioned above, details of other important writings on the recorder by Carl Dolmetsch are as follows:

'The Recorder or English Flute.' *Music & Letters* Vol. 22, no. 1 (January 1941) pp. 67-74.

'On Playing the Recorder.' *The Consort* 7 (July 1950) pp. 18-21

'The Recorder and Flute.' *The Consort* 14 (July 1957) pp. 18-23.

'The Recorder and German Flute during the 17th and 18th Centuries.' *Proceedings of the Royal Musical Association* 83 (1957) pp. 49-63.

'Which Way to Turn the Clock?' *Recorder & Music Magazine* Vol. 2 no. 9 (May 1968) pp. 283-284.
(A defence of alterations to the design of the modern recorder, such as the addition of bell and lip keys and modifications to the bore, to adapt the instrument to suit present-day performing conditions).

'Is There Magic in Wood?' *Recorder & Music Magazine* Vol. 3 no. 6 (June 1970) p. 217.
(Considers that choice of wood has little bearing on a recorder's tone).

'High F Sharp.' *The Recorder & Music Magazine* Vol.8 no.9 (March 1986) p. 275.
(Describes the method of slurred fingering to obtain high F# and the discovery that stopping the bell enabled the production of the note. Recounts the invention of the bell key).

'This will be very useful to me.' in *A Birthday Album for the Society of Recorder Players*, Forsyth (1987) pp. 82-84.
(Describes Arnold Dolmetsch's purchase of the famous Bressan recorder, Carl's involvement in its loss, Arnold's construction of a replacement, and the eventual finding and return of the original. Continues with a brief history of the subsequent revival and development of the recorder in the 20th century).

'The Recorder in Evolution.' *The Recorder Magazine* Vol.16 no. 2 (June 1996) pp. 55-56.
(A survey of the various devices Carl had introduced to the modern recorder – bell key, lip key etc).

Carl Dolmetsch: **A Centenary Celebration**

THE WIGMORE HALL RECITALS 1939-1989

Carl Dolmetsch and Joseph Saxby's recital given in the Wigmore Hall on 1st February 1939 was one of the most significant events in the recorder's 20th-century revival. Recorder consort music had been included in concerts at the Haslemere Festival since its inauguration in 1925, but the Wigmore Hall recital was almost certainly the first devoted entirely to the recorder as a solo instrument. Significantly, the souvenir programme and notes (a number of pages of which are reproduced here) included a brief history of the recorder and a note on its modern revival. The works performed were almost entirely from the 18th century, but also included was the first performance of Carl's own *Theme and Variations in A minor* for descant recorder and harpsichord, composed the previous year. He had been keen to include a contemporary work for recorder, but in the absence of the sort of piece he was seeking, performed his own; a bold move, since he was by his own admission neither an accomplished nor acknowledged composer. But the message it sent out was obvious and unequivocal - that the instrument need not be confined to the repertoire of its past.

Carl Dolmetsch: **A Centenary Celebration**

WIGMORE HALL

Wednesday, February 1st, 1939
at 8.15 p.m.

RECORDER RECITAL
(English Flute)

CARL F. DOLMETSCH

Assisted by

JOSEPH SAXBY — Harpsichord

IBBS & TILLETT
124, Wigmore St., W.1

Souvenir
PROGRAMME & NOTES
Price: 1/-
Copyright. All rights reserved.

Cover of the souvenir programme for Carl Dolmetsch's first Wigmore Hall recital

THE RECORDER or ENGLISH FLUTE

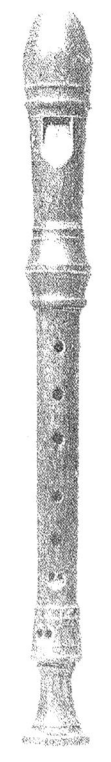

This delightful wood-wind instrument is of simple appearance, having no keys, except on the largest instruments where the stretch is too great for the hand. There are eight holes, seven in the front, and one thumb-hole at the back. On most modern instruments the two lower holes are double, giving clearer semitones in the lower register. The English Flute has a chromatic range of well over two octaves, and can be played in any key with the utmost ease.

It is noted for the purity of its tone, which in the hands of a master offers great powers of *crescendo* and *decrescendo*, without loss of good intonation. This is one of the finest points of Recorder technique. The novice trying to increase the tone invariably overblows, going sharp, or attempts a *pianissimo* by underblowing, with consequent flatness of pitch. The tone, in spite of its mellowness, is very penetrating. This characteristic enables it to meet the demands of both concert hall and music room. The subtle inflections are infinite: there is a telling warmth in *cantabile* passages, whilst the instantaneous response to quick tonguing is unexcelled, lending to *staccato* a piquancy and freshness seldom heard to-day.

The Recorder music reveals, when played in complete form with the correct ornamentation, cadenzas, and interpretation based on contemporary evidence, that the highest degree of technical ability is required. Although virtuosity should not be worshipped as an end in itself, it is an essential part of the true artist's equipment. The comparative ease with which beginners arrive at the playing of simple tunes may lead one to underestimate the rich rewards this instrument will yield in the hands of the artist-virtuoso.

THE MODERN REVIVAL OF THE RECORDER, like that of the Harpsichord, is an accomplished fact. At intervals during the last 150 years antiquarians have taken old instruments from museums and private collections, played upon them, without a proper study of the correct fingering as set out in the treatises which survive, and then have wondered how their forebears could have endured such "bad intonation"! Until Arnold Dolmetsch made his first researches into this subject in 1903, no one had seriously studied the proper technique and music of the instrument with more than antiquarian curiosity.

In 1918-19 Arnold Dolmetsch produced his first modern Recorders, and in 1925, the first modern consort of Recorders, with bass, was heard at Haslemere. From this sprang the enthusiasm which spread throughout Germany, and subsequently all over the world.

The early triumphs of the Recorder were followed in brilliant succession by the discovery and performance of consorts, obbligati, Sonatas and Concerti, by such famous masters as Bach, Handel, Purcell, Telemann, and Loeillet. These established for the Recorder its rightful place in the world of music; not as an antiquarian curiosity, nor yet to replace any modern instrument, but as a living vital resource. Does not an instrument, for which these masters wrote some of their finest works, merit the attention of the artist and composer of to-day? This view was clearly expressed by Mr. J. A. Westrup, writing from Haslemere in the *Daily Telegraph* and *Morning Post*, on July 19th, 1938 :—"These winning instruments are unjustly neglected to-day. A composer who would write a quartet for them instead of wringing painful novelty from trumpet or violin, could earn no small gratitude."

Second page of the souvenir programme for Carl Dolmetsch's first Wigmore Hall recital

BIOGRAPHICAL SKETCH by H. E. Wortham

CARL DOLMETSCH
Photo by Elliott & Fry

Mr. CARL DOLMETSCH, who is giving the first Recorder Recital ever held in a London hall, on February 1st, 1939, has been a master of that instrument since the age of 15. As is natural for a son of Mr. Arnold Dolmetsch, his musical education began at a very early age. When he was four he was already receiving lessons from his father in the best traditions of the 18th Century masters of the craft.

Carl Dolmetsch has devoted his scholarship and inherited skill to the renaissance of the instrument which Shakespeare knew so well. He has explored its literature, and either alone or in a consort of Recorders has given the musical public on both sides of the Atlantic opportunities of judging its beauties. A year or two ago his recitals in America were acclaimed by the critics as opening windows on a new world of music.

Carl Dolmetsch is an example of the cosmopolitan influences which have contributed to the art of nearly all the great composers from John Sebastian Bach downwards. He has sprung from a family who were for generations burghers of Zurich. His father, the octogenarian Arnold Dolmetsch, has an international reputation for his revival of the Viols and other early instruments. On his mother's side Carl Dolmetsch has also inherited strong artistic traditions.

His uncle, the late Sir Harry Johnston, in addition to being a pioneer of Empire in East and Central Africa and first Special Commissioner for Uganda, was himself a brilliant artist. Mrs. Dolmetsch is highly talented as an artist as well as a musician. Carl has reinforced the Scottish-French alliance of his parents by marrying a niece of Viscount Weir. They live at Haslemere, and when he is not travelling about the country concert-giving, he devotes his energies to carrying on the work which Mr. Arnold Dolmetsch, owing to his advanced years, has now to leave largely to his family and disciples.

Though born in France, Carl Dolmetsch followed the family tradition in adopting Swiss nationality. In 1931, however, he became a British subject; he speaks both English and French perfectly.

Biographical sketch of Carl Dolmetsch in the souvenir programme for his first Wigmore Hall recital

The Wigmore Hall Recitals 1939-1989

PROGRAMME

1. SONATA in C MINOR, for Descant Recorder and Harpsichord
   J. B. Senaille le Fils
   (Ordinaire de la Chambre de Musique du Roi Louis XIV. et XV.)

   Preludio—Adagio.   Corrente.   Gavotta.   Giga.
   (Accompaniment by A. Dolmetsch from original Figured Bass)

2. SONATA in F MAJOR, Op. 1, No. 11, for Treble Recorder and Harpsichord   *G. F. Handel*

   Larghetto.   Allegro.   Sicilliana.   Giga.
   (Accompaniment by Rudolph Dolmetsch from Figured Bass)

3. SONATA quasi una Fantasia, Op. 27, No. 2, ("The Moonlight Sonata")   *L. van Beethoven*

   Adagio sostenuto.   Allegretto.   Presto agitato.

INTERVAL.

4. THEME and VARIATIONS in A minor for Descant Recorder and Harpsichord   *Carl F. Dolmetsch*
   (1938)

5. SONATA in C MINOR, for Treble Recorder and Harpsichord   *J. B. L'Oeillet de Gant*
   (1653—1728)

   Largo.   Allegro.   Poco allegro.   Adagio Giga.
   (Accompaniment by C. F. Dolmetsch from original Figured Bass)

6. GROUP of PIECES :

   a. Andante and Two Menuets in E minor, for Descant Recorder and Harpsichord   *J. M. le Clair*
   (1738)
   (Accompaniment by C. F. Dolmetsch from Figured Bass)

   b. Chaconne in F major, for Treble Recorder   ...   *Henry Purcell*
   (Accompaniment by Arnold Dolmetsch)

   c. Two Menuets in C major   ...   .   *J. S. Bach*
   III. 6. IV.

Some of the above works and others are obtainable on Columbia and Dolmetsch Gramophone Records.

Harpsichord and Recorders by Dolmetsch of Haslemere.

Programme of Carl Dolmetsch's first Wigmore Hall recital

JOSEPH SAXBY

JOSEPH SAXBY has worked under Mr. Arnold Dolmetsch himself at Haslemere, making a special study of correct ornamentation and Harpsichord registration. He has collaborated in concerts with members of the Dolmetsch family since 1932, and appeared at the Haslemere Festival, with which his name is now associated.

The only son of Michael Zacharewitsch the celebrated violinist, he toured America with his father at the age of 15. He now uses his mother's name to avoid professional confusion with his father's musical reputation.

Mr. Saxby and Mr. Carl F. Dolmetsch have worked together a great deal, with a view to attaining perfect unity of musical purpose.

Profile of Joseph Saxby in the programme of his first recital with Carl Dolmetsch at the Wigmore Hall

On 18th November 1939 Carl gave a second Wigmore Hall recital joined, as will be seen from the reproduced pages of the programme, by Christopher Wood, Joseph Saxby having been prevented from taking part by his Civil Defence Duties. Again the programme featured music mainly from the 17th and 18th centuries, but Carl also gave the first public performance of Lennox Berkeley's *Sonatina* for treble recorder and harpsichord, having already given a private performance at a studio meeting of the London Contemporary Music Centre in June 1939. Included in the printed programme (and also reproduced here) was a short article entitled 'The Future of the Recorder' not attributed to, but almost certainly written by Carl. Of the ten new recorder works noted as having been completed, those by Christian Darnton and Eve Kisch were withdrawn, and that by Britten would appear not to have progressed beyond the most preliminary sketches, if indeed at all, as he sailed for the USA in April 1939. However, the remaining seven were subsequently published (Rawsthorne's *Suite* not until 1994) and represent among the first serious attempts to compose contemporary music for the recorder. The Sonatinas by Lennox Berkeley and Walter Leigh in particular have retained their popularity and continue to be frequently performed.

WIGMORE HALL

SATURDAY, NOVEMBER 18th, 1939
at 3.15 p.m.

RECORDER RECITAL

(English Flute)

CARL F. DOLMETSCH

Assisted by

CHRISTOPHER WOOD

Harpsichord

IBBS & TILLETT
124, Wigmore Street, W.1

Souvenir
PROGRAMME & NOTES
Price: 1/-
Copyright. All rights reserved.

Cover of the souvenir programme for Carl Dolmetsch's second Wigmore Hall recital

Carl Dolmetsch: **A Centenary Celebration**

THE FUTURE OF THE RECORDER

It was the conspicuous lack of good contemporary Recorder music which prompted Mr. Carl Dolmetsch to give the lead in February of this year when he wrote and performed his Theme and Variations for Solo Recorder and Harpsichord. To-day, nine months later, the situation has radically changed as may be seen from the following report which appeared in the *Daily Telegraph and Morning Post* when Mr. Dolmetsch had played at a Studio Concert of the London Contemporary Music Centre in June : " The Recorder has hitherto been associated with the revival of music of the 17th and 18th centuries. At the London Contemporary Music Centre's Studio meeting on Saturday afternoon we learnt how it could serve the composer to-day.

" The result was encouraging. Provided that an instrument is mechanically perfect—as the modern Recorder is—there is clearly no reason why it should be confined to the music of the past . . . . Purcell, Telemann, and Loeillet. These established for the Recorder its rightful place in the world of music ; not as an antiquarian curiosity, nor yet to replace any modern instrument, but as a living, vital resource. Does not an instrument for which these masters wrote some of their finest works, merit the attention of the artist and composer of to-day ? This view was clearly expressed by Mr. J. A. Westrup, writing from Haslemere in the *Daily Telegraph and Morning Post*, on July 19th, 1938 :—" These winning instruments are unjustly neglected to-day. A composer who would write a quartet for them instead of wringing painful novelty from trumpet or violin, could earn no small gratitude."

" Not all the composers represented in Saturday's programme had thoroughly grasped either the character or the technique of the instrument.

" But the concert as a whole proved a serious intention to establish and justify the relationship between this seductive instrument and the music of our time. The most successful of the works for Treble Recorder was Lennox Berkeley's Sonatina. Its apparent simplicity concealed a neat and attractive invention and the solo instrument sounded completely at home with the material."

J. A. W.

It was the general appreciation, coupled with Mr. Carl Dolmetsch's personal enjoyment and esteem of Mr. Berkeley's Sonatina at this private hearing, which decided him to give the work its first public performance at the Wigmore Hall to-day.

Acknowledgments and thanks are due to Mr. Manuel Jacobs, himself a Recorder player and composer for that instrument, for his enterprise in personally bringing to the notice of ten composers of the younger British school the tempting resources offered by the Recorder in a new field of operation. As a result of his efforts, ten new sonatinas (the Lennox Berkeley amongst them) have been written and this collection is shortly to be published under the editorship of Mr. Jacobs.

The foregoing will substantiate the view that an instrument like the Recorder, which can live on its own merits irrespective of age, will surely be given a future besides a distinguished past and present. Other living composers who have already succumbed to its charm and possibilities include Hindemith, Benjamin Britten, Stanley Bate and Alan Rawsthorne.

The Recorder enthusiast now has something new to turn to, and he may well be assured of more to come.

NOTE: If you have enjoyed this Recital and would like to hear of future Dolmetsch Concerts, please sign the Visitors Book at the door, or write to the Concert Secretary, " Jesses," Haslemere, Surrey.

'The Future of the recorder' from the programme of Carl Dolmetsch's second Wigmore Hall Recital

The Wigmore Hall Recitals 1939-1989

PROGRAMME

1. SUITE in G, for Descant Recorder and Harpsichord
   De Caix d'Hervelois
   (1736)

   Prélude. "La Christine." Sarabande. "La Tubeuf."

   (Accompaniment by C. F. DOLMETSCH from Figured Bass)

2. SONATA in C MAJOR, for Treble Recorder and Harpsichord .. .. .. *G. F. Handel*

   Larghetto. Allegro. "A tempo di Gavotti." Allegro.

   (Accompaniment by RUDOLPH DOLMETSCH from Figured Bass)

3. FANTASIA in C MINOR for the Harpsichord *W. A. Mozart*
   (1785)

   INTERVAL.

4. SONATINA in A for Treble Recorder and Harpsichord .. .. .. *Lennox Berkeley*
   (1939)

   Moderato. Adagio. Allegro. Moderato.

5. GROUP OF BIRD PIECES:

   a. "The Goldfinch" .. .. *Ben. Cosyns*
   (c. 1600)

   *b. "Le Rossignol en amour"
   c. "Double du Rossignol"
   F. Couperin
   (1722)

   (Accompaniments by A. and C. F. DOLMETSCH)

6. SONATA in C MAJOR for Treble Recorder and Harpsichord .. .. *G. Ph. Telemann*
   (1681-1767)

   Cantabile. Allegro. Grave. Vivace.

   * The Nightingale in Love.

Records of Mr. Dolmetsch's playing are available only on lists of COLUMBIA and DOLMETSCH RECORDING.

Harpsichord and Recorders by DOLMETSCH of Haslemere.

NOTE.—Mr. Joseph Saxby, who was originally to have assisted Mr. Dolmetsch in the above programme and also to have played Mozart's C minor Fantasia, unfortunately has been prevented from doing so by his Civil Defence Duties in London. Christopher Wood, having also worked a great deal with Carl Dolmetsch in Haslemere, and recently accompanying him on a concert tour in the North, has agreed to replace Mr. Saxby.

Programme of Carl Dolmetsc's second Wigmore Hall recital

(The footnote explains Joseph Saxby's abence and replacement by Christopher Wood)

Joseph Saxby's enforced absence from the second Wigmore Hall recital and the moving forward of commencement to 3.15 p.m. (and thus into daylight hours) were symptomatic of the onset of World War II and the effect this was to have on the continuing revival of the recorder. However, In June 1945 Manuel Jacobs wrote to Carl suggesting he recommence his Wigmore Hall recitals, and the following year, taking a lead from Jacobs, Carl approached York Bowen and requested a new work for recorder. Bowen's *Sonatina* was premiered at the Wigmore Hall on 28th May 1947 with the composer at the piano. There was no new work included in the 1948 recital, but in May 1949 Carl and Joseph gave the first performance of Edmund Rubbra's *Meditazioni sopra 'Cœurs désolés'*, considered by many to be among the finest works for recorder of the 20th century.

For the next forty years Carl gave an annual Wigmore Hall recital, all of which, except that of 1952 when he gave a repeat performance of Berkeley's *Sonatina*, included the performance of a new work. At six recitals two new works were premiered, and on one occasion, in 1973, no fewer than three. A list of Wigmore premieres is included below. To emphasise that the new works were not simply occasional pieces Carl frequently reprogrammed performances of several of his favourites at subsequent Wigmore Hall recitals. One such was York Bowen's *Sonatina* which was played, as at its premiere, with Bowen at the piano in the recital on 8th February 1960. For this Bowen wrote a short programme note, the original of which, in Bowen's hand, is in the Dolmetsch archives. A facsimile is included below. It is interesting to observe that Bowen gave the title of the work as *Sonata*. At the time the work was composed the title seemed to create uncertainty, Bowen referring to it both as *Sonata* and *Sonatina* in correspondence. This is reflected in the autograph manuscript, the score of which is headed *Sonata*, while the recorder part is headed *Sonatina*.

25, LANGLAND GARDENS,
LONDON. N.W.3.
TELEPHONE: HAMPSTEAD 8347.

Sonata for Recorder and Piano

York Bowen. Opus 121.

Moderato.
Andante tranquillo
Allegro giocoso

This work is in three short movements, the first of which is in conventional Sonata form with two themes and a short section of development. The music moves gently and leans to the lyrical in style. The second and slower movement remains tranquil in mood and is very free in form. The last movement demands a quick change of recorder from the previous Treble in F to the smaller Descant model in C which, like the Piccolo to the Flute, sounds an octave higher than actually written. In this Finale the music is completely different to the preceding and shows the more brilliant and agile possibilities of this very effective instrument. This movement might well be termed "Scherzo-Finale".

Y.B.

York Bowen's programme note for the 1960 Wigmore Hall performance of his Sonatina

Carl Dolmetsch: A Centenary Celebration

Many other musicians besides Joseph Saxby joined Carl at these recitals, and this is reflected in the scoring of many of the new works. In 1955 the Martin String Quartet was engaged for the premiere of Rubbra's *Fantasia on a Theme of Machaut* and took part in a further six Wigmore Hall recitals including the premiere of Gordon Jacob's *Suite* for recorder and string quartet in 1958. Other distinguished musicians included the soprano Elizabeth Harwood, the brothers Anthony and Kerry Camden (oboe and bassoon), Robert Spencer (lute), the percussionist James Blades, John Mills (guitar) and John Orford (bassoon). During his USA tours in the early 1960s Carl met violinist and cellist sisters Alice and Eleonore Schoenfeld. They took part in five Wigmore Hall recitals, and played in the premiers of Arnold Cooke's *Quartet*, Hans Gál's *Trio Serenade*, John Gardner's *Concerto da camera*, Joseph Horovitz's *Quartetto concertante* (sadly later withdrawn by the composer) and Francis Chagrin's *Preludes for Four*.

Eleonare and Alice Schoenfeld with Joseph Saxby and Carl Dolmetsch at a rehearsal in the 1960s

Carl's Wigmore Hall recital on 27th October 1989 was a particularly special occasion marking the fiftieth anniversary of the two he had given in 1939. He was joined by Sir David Lumsden on the harpsichord (Joseph Saxby had played in his last Wigmore Hall recital in 1986, but was present in the audience on this occasion) and by the Chamber Orchestra of the Royal Academy of Music. The programme for this recital is reproduced below, from which it will be seen that the final item was Gordon Jacob's *Suite* in the version with small string orchestra. Sadly this was Carl's last Wigmore Hall recital - a remarkable era had come to an end, one that had included the premieres of some of the most significant new works for recorder in the 20th century.

The Wigmore Hall Recitals 1939-1989

WIGMORE HALL
36 Wigmore Street, W1H 9DF

Friday, 27th October, 1989
at 7.30 p.m.

RECORDER RECITAL
CARL DOLMETSCH

with

SIR DAVID LUMSDEN — Harpsichord

and

THE CHAMBER ORCHESTRA OF THE ROYAL ACADEMY
Leader: Martin Burgess

Manager: William Lyne, M.B.E.
Lessees: Westminster City Council

Souvenir
Programme & Notes

Cover of the souvenir programme for Carl Dolmetsch's last Wigmore Hall recital

Carl Dolmetsch: A Centenary Celebration

1939-1989

To mark the 50th year since Carl Dolmetsch gave the first solo recorder recital in history, at the Wigmore Hall, he is partnered by Sir David Lumsden at the harpsichord and The Chamber Orchestra of the Royal Academy. During the course of a distinguished career, Carl Dolmetsch's global tours have encompassed the American Continents (including Alaska and Canada), most European countries, and Australia, New Zealand and Japan.

Carl Dolmetsch's supreme artistry has inspired British and foreign composers of repute to dedicate works to him and in 1953 H.M. The Queen appointed him C.B.E. for his services to music. Alone among artists of his standing, Carl Dolmetsch designs and makes his own instruments; he has also discovered, transcribed and edited for performance many of the works in his extensive repertoire.

1939 PRESS REVIEWS

"... Wigmore Hall full ... Carl Dolmetsch, who has been brought up in the soundest traditions of interpretation and has also acquired an unequalled mastery of the instrument *(recorder)*. The special interest of this recital lay not only in the display of technical skill, but in the way in which phrasing, rhythm and expression were chosen to suit the music. The cadenzas, too, had an authentic ring ... But 18th century style can be achieved by a musician who has soaked himself in it, as Mr. Dolmetsch proved in his own "Theme and Variations" in A minor. Here there was both an expert reconstruction of the manner of the past, and also a challenge to virtuosity which few besides the composer would care to accept. Mr. Dolmetsch made it all sound child's play, so that it was easy to revel with him in the skips and scamperings". — J.A. Westrup, *The Daily Telegraph*.

"... anything tongued is delicious, and the intonation is astonishingly good ... Mr. Dolmetsch's playing of a Sonata by Handel and another of Loeillet, of Purcell and Bach and a short bit of Telemann was extremely delicate ... after hearing this English Flute *(recorder)* played with the incomparable skill and musicianship of Mr. Dolmetsch, one no longer wonders why a not inconsiderable number of modern composers wish to write for it". — *The Observer*.

"Mr. Carl Dolmetsch has put the English Flute *(recorder)* ... once more on the map of modern music". — *The Times*

"The recorder, or English Flute, is an instrument of lovely tone, and Mr. Dolmetsch is its recognised virtuoso ... *(he)* played a number of works to the great content and pleasure of the audience ... a pleasant and unusual concert." — J.A. Forsyth, *The Star*.

"Mr. Carl Dolmetsch attracted a large and keenly interested audience to his recital ... Mr. Dolmetsch's phenomenal virtuosity was displayed in his own Theme and Variations in A minor for the descant recorder ... it was an achievement for Mr. Carl Dolmetsch, whose skill upon the recorder is unequalled anywhere today". — *The Musical Times*.

PROGRAMME

This recital is sponsored by a Governor of the Dolmetsch Foundation.

Sonata in F major for treble recorder, strings and harpsichord

    Allegro moderato   Fuga allegro   Grave   Menuetto allegro   *A. Scarlatti 1659-1725*

The original MS of this work is preserved in the University of Münster Library. As an example of fluent technique and invention in the concerto grosso *genre* it compares with that of Corelli and Handel; Scarlatti's style is, however, unmistakable, displaying too a thorough knowledge of writing for recorder with string accompaniment. The Sonata opens with a bustling Allegro, followed by a fully worked out Fugue. The Grave calls for expressive ornamentation from the recorder linking the chordal passages of the strings. The work concludes with a playful allegro in 3/8 time featuring lively exchanges between recorder and violins.

Second page of the souvenir programme for Carl Dolmetsch's last Wigmore Hall recital

Solo pieces for various recorders

"Plaint"	*(tenor)*	*Colin Hand*
Variations on a theme by Herbert Howells	*(descant)*	*Alan Ridout*
"Tempo di Gavotta"	*(bass)*	*Carl Dolmetsch*
Air in the Lydian Mode from "Sequence"	*(sopranino)*	*Alan Ridout*

Originally written as a "New Year Offering" for Carl Dolmetsch, Colin Hand's rhapsodical "Plaint" calls for the expressive tone of the tenor recorder, serving as a reminder that its potential tends to be overlooked by modern writers.

Herbert Howells' theme originally entitled "Pipe Tune" was composed for his student Anne Lawrence. Ruth Dyson (her contemporary) later wrote it down from memory for Alan Ridout, who composed the Variations receiving their first public performance today.

Prompted by the scarcity of solo music for bass recorder, Carl Dolmetsch has written this lively Gavotte exploiting the entire compass of the instrument, displaying a range far wider than is usually met with in consort playing.

Alan Ridout's "Sequence" for recorder and lute was first performed by Carl Dolmetsch and Robert Spencer in the Wigmore Hall in 1975. "Air in the Lydian Mode" comes sixth in the set and, with the composer's concurrence, is effectively played on sopranino recorder accompanied by the plucked sonority of the harpsichord.

French Suite No. 1 in D minor (BWV812) for solo harpsichord

Allemande   Courante   Sarabande   Menuets I & II   Gigue

J.S. Bach 1685-1750

Composed when Bach was Capellmeister to the Prince of Cöthen, and during his most fertile period of instrumental writing, the so-called "French Suites" date from *circa* 1723. While the titles to the various movements are predominantly French and the style of the music itself is obviously French influenced, it is doubtful whether the popular appellation originated with Bach; it is probable that the terms "English" and "French" served to distinguish the sets of keyboard suites. Indeed, this would seem to be borne out by a note in Johann Christian's own ms copy of the English Suites: *"Fait pour les Anglois"* (sic) The first three French Suites are in minor keys and the second three in major, the former being generally pensive and elegiac in character. The well-known Sarabande in the present Suite is one of Bach's most sublime and profound moments; exceptionally, the Gigue is in common time, suggesting a quicker version of the *grave* section of a French *Ouverture*.

Suite in A minor for treble recorder, strings and harpsichord

Ouverture (Lento-Allegro-Lento)	"Rejouissance" (Presto)
"Les Plaisirs" (Presto)	Passpieds I & II
"Air à l'Italien" (Largo-Allegro-Largo)	Polonaise
Menuets I & II	

G.P. Telemann 1681-1767

Telemann's A minor Suite has an international flavour, with its traditional French *"Ouverture"*, quixotic *"Air à l'Italien"* and spirited *"Polonaise"*, interspersed with typical French dance movements. The writing throughout is skilfully contrived to suit quartet or orchestra equally, in either case achieving a good balance with the solo recorder. For tonal variety, there are passages for recorder, harpsichord and cello and others for strings alone.

INTERVAL

Sonata Sesta in A minor for treble recorder, with harpsichord and cello

Largo   Allegro   Allegro   Vivace

Francesco Maria Veracini 1690-1768

Veracini's twelve *Sonate a Flauto o Violino solo e Basso* published in 1716 precede by five years his better-known "Opus I" — *Twelve Sonatas for Violin and Bass* printed in 1721. The earlier set was dedicated to Prince Friedrich August of Saxony in whose service Veracini was at that time. The recorder (designated *Flauto*) was then much in vogue in both Italy and Germany, and the style and range of the *Sonate* are well suited to this instrument. Like his uncle, Antonio, Francesco enjoyed a tremendous reputation as composer and performer: even the legendary Tartini was so impressed as to retire from public performance for a year to improve his own playing. The work has been transcribed and edited by Carl Dolmetsch from the Dolmetsch Library copy, and the harpsichord part was written out from the original figured bass by Joseph Saxby *(Universal Edition 14008)*.

Third page of the souvenir programme for Carl Dolmetsch's last Wigmore Hall recital

Carl Dolmetsch: **A Centenary Celebration**

Concerto in G major for descant recorder, strings and harpsichord
    Allegro   Adagio   Allegro   *Jean-Jacques Naudot c.1710-1769*

A protegé of Count Egmont, Jean-Jacques Naudot was one of the most celebrated virtuosi of his day. His considerable output for wind instruments includes a set of Six Concertos, Opus XVII, dating from 1740, from which the present work is taken. The two outer movements are brisk and cheerful, while the Adagio (in G minor) begins and ends with dramatic double-dotted tuttis on a Purcellian chromatic bass contrasting with the lyrical solo writing for the recorder.

Suite for treble recorder and string orchestra

Prelude	Pavane
English Dance	Introduction and Cadenza
Lamento	Tarantella
Burlesca alla Rumba	

Gordon Jacob

This Suite was given its first performance by Carl Dolmetsch and the Martin String Quartet in the Wigmore Hall on 31st January 1958. Gordon Jacob contributed the following programme note:-

"This Suite, which was written towards the end of 1957, is dedicated to Carl Dolmetsch, in whose hands the recorder has become an instrument possessing a great range of colour and expressiveness and also brilliant technical virtuosity. A number of contemporary British composers have written works for recorder which have shown that it is by no means restricted to the interpretation of old music, but can also respond to the exacting demands of the present day.

The Prelude, Lament and Pavane in this Suite are quiet and contemplative in mood in contrast with the other movements, which are brisk and rhythmical. The Burlesca alla Rumba belongs, as its name suggests, to the category of parody, but it is written affectionately rather than satirically. The Cadenza is a kind of improvisatory rumination on the themes of the pieces which precede it. In the introduction to this movement, the 'cello plays an important part. In the final movement (Tarantella) the composer recommends the alternative use of the sopranino recorder, which bears the same relation to the treble recorder as the piccolo does to the flute, i.e. it has the same fingering, but sounds an octave higher than the written notes. The composer has provided an *ad libitum* Double Bass part, so that the Suite can be played with a small string orchestra if so desired".

CHAMBER ORCHESTRA

Violin	**Viola**	**Cello**
Martin Burgess *(leader)*	Nikos Zarb	Paul Brunner
Lucy Gould	Esther Goddard	Martin Storey
Clare Howick		
Clare Hayes		
Nicola Burton		**Bass**
Harriet Rayfield		Dawn Baker

No Smoking in the auditorium.

No recording or photographic equipment may be taken into the auditorium, nor used in any other part of the Hall without the prior written consent of the Hall management.

In accordance with the requirements of Westminster City Council — Persons shall not be permitted to stand or sit in any of the gangways. If standing is permitted in the gangway at the rear of the seating, it shall be limited to the number indicated in the notice exhibited.

The Wigmore Hall is equiped with a 'Loop' to help hearing aid users receive clear sound without background noise. Patrons can use this facility by switching their hearing aids over to 'T'.

★ ★ ★ ★ ★ ★ ★ ★ ★ ★ ★

The Dolmetsch Years
A Festival and Exhibition to Celebrate the Life and Work
of the Pioneer Arnold Dolmetsch, on the 50th Anniversary
of his Death, and the first Hundred Years of the Early Music Renaissance

St. John's Smith Square, London
22-29 May 1990

Booking opens 1 March, 1990
Under the auspices of the Dolmetsch Foundation

Management: David Stone Associates Limited, Great Dowles, Stone Street, Canterbury, Kent CT4 6DB.
Tel: 0227 87355.
Management reserves the right to alter programmes and artists.

Printed by:
Blackdown Press Ltd
Haslemere, Surrey

Fourth (final) page of the souvenir programme for Carl Dolmetsch's last Wigmore Hall recital

(Note the advertisement for the festival and exhibition 'The Dolmetsch Years' to be held at St John's Smith Square the following year to mark the fiftieth anniversary of Arnold Dolmetsch's death)

New works performed by Carl Dolmetsch at his Wigmore Hall recitals 1939-1989

Year	Composer	Title	Scoring	Publisher
1939	Carl Dolmetsch	*Theme and Variations in A minor*	tr rec & hpd	Peacock
1939	Lennox Berkeley	*Sonatina*	tr rec & kbd	Schott
1947	York Bowen	*Sonatina*	rec (tr/desc) & pn	Emerson Edition
1949	Edmund Rubbra	*Meditazioni sopra 'Cœurs désolés'*	tr rec & kbd	Lengnick
1950	Herbert Murrill	*Sonata*	tr rec & kbd	Peacock (OUP)
1952	Cyril Scott	*Aubade*	tr rec & kbd	Schott
1953	Antony Hopkins	*Suite*	desc rec & pn	Schott
1954	Norman Fulton	*Scottish Suite*	tr rec & kbd	Schott
1955	Edmund Rubbra	*Fantasia on a Theme of Machaut*	tr rec, str qt & hpd	Lengnick
1956	Lennox Berkeley	*Concertino*	tr rec, vln, vc & hpd	J W Chester
1957	Edmund Rubbra	*Cantata pastorale*	high voice, tr rec, vc & hpd	Lengnick
1958	Gordon Jacob	*Suite*	tr rec & str qt (or str orch)	Peacock (OUP)
1959	Robert Simpson	*Variations and Fugue*	tr rec & str qt	Peacock
1960	Arnold Cooke	*Divertimento*	tr rec & str qt (or str orch)	MS-unpublished
1961	Georges Migot	*Sonatine*	desc rec & pn	Bärenreiter
1961	Alan Hovhaness	*Sextet*	tr rec, str qt & hpd	Fujihara
1962	Edmund Rubbra	*Passacaglia sopra 'Plusieurs regrets'*	tr rec & kbd	Lengnick
1962	Hans Gál	*Concertino*	tr rec & str qt (or str orch)	Universal Edition
1963	Gordon Jacob	*Variations*	tr rec & kbd	Musica Rara
1964	John Gardner	*Little Suite in C*	tr rec & kbd	Anglo American
1965	Arnold Cooke	*Quartet (Sonata)*	tr rec, vln, vc & hpd	Schott
1965	Edmund Rubbra	*Sonatina*	tr rec & hpd	Lengnick
1966	Richard Arnell	*Quintet (The Gambian)*	tr rec & str qt	Peacock
1966	Nigel Butterley	*The White-Throated Warbler*	s'nino rec & hpd	Orpheus Music
1967	Hans Gál	*Trio Serenade*	tr rec, vln & vc	Simrock
1968	John Gardner	*Concerto da camera*	tr rec, vln, vc & hpd	The composer
1969	Joseph Horovitz	*Quartetto concertante (withdrawn)*	tr rec, vln, vc & hpd	-
1970	Francis Chagrin	*Preludes for Four*	tr rec, vln, vc & hpd	Novello
1971	Stephen Dodgson	*Warbeck Dances*	rec (s'nino/tr) & hpd	Peacock
1972	Nicholas Maw	*Discourse*	tr rec & hpd	MS-unpublished
1972	Walter Bergmann	*Pastorella*	sop voice & s'nino rec	Magnamusic
1973	Arnold Cooke	*Suite*	desc, tr & t recs, optional hpd	Moeck
1973	Gordon Jacob	*A Consort of Recorders*	desc, tr, t & b recs	MS-unpublished
1973	Martin Dalby	*Páginas*	tr rec & hpd	Novello
1974	Hans Gál	*Three Intermezzi*	tr rec & kbd	Schott
1974	William Mathias	*Concertino*	tr rec, ob, bn & hpd	OUP
1975	Alan Ridout	*Sequence*	tr rec & lute	Peacock
1976	Malcolm Lipkin	*Interplay*	tr rec, perc, gamba & hpd	The composer
1977	Alun Hoddinott	*Italian Suite*	tr rec & gui	OUP
1978	Edmund Rubbra	*Fantasia on a Chord*	tr rec, hpd & optional gamba	Lengnick
1979	Lennox Berkeley	*Cantata 'Una and the Lion'*	S sop voice, rec hpd & gamba	J J W Chester
1980	Michael Berkeley	*American Suite*	tr rec & bn	OUP
1981	Alan Ridout	*Chamber Concerto*	tr rec & str qt	Peacock
1982	Donald Swann	*Rhapsody from Within*	rec (tr/t) & kbd	Peacock
1983	Gordon Jacob	*Suite (Trifles)*	tr rec, vln, vc & hpd	Emerson Edition
1984	Colin Hand	*Concerto cantico (withdrawn)*	tr rec & str qt	-
1985	Michael Short	*Sinfonia*	tr rec, str qt & hpd	MS-unpublished
1986	Arnold Cooke	*Divertimento*	desc and tr recs, vln, vc & hpd	MS-unpublished
1987	Lionel Salter	*Air and Dance*	tr rec & pn	MS-unpublished
1988	Jean Françaix	*Quintette*	tr rec, 2 vln & hpd	Schott
1989	Alan Ridout	*Variants on a Tune of H.H.*	desc rec & hpd	Peacock

Carl Dolmetsch: **A Centenary Celebration**

A WEALTH OF IMPORTANT CORRESPONDENCE

The Dolmetsch archives contain literally hundreds of letters exchanged between Carl and many of the musicians with whom he worked. Of special interest is the correspondence with the composers who wrote new works for him, in which it is frequently possible to trace the history of a piece from Carl's initial contact with the composer, through to the first performance and sometimes beyond. Some letters deal with practical things such as the arrangements for rehearsals (which are interesting in that they reveal the composer's involvement at this stage), but others give a unique insight into the way a piece developed.

Carl's long friendship with Edmund Rubbra is reflected in the many letters they exchanged, and resulted in the premieres of six new works at the Wigmore Hall. The first of these was *Meditazioni sopra 'Cœurs désolés* in 1949. Edgar Hunt initially suggested that Rubbra's interest in early music might make him sympathetic to the idea of composing contemporary works for the recorder. Carl evidently contacted him with a request for a new work and received the letter reproduced in facsimile below.

VALLEY COTTAGE.
SPEEN.
AYLESBURY, BUCKS.
TEL. HAMPDEN ROW 69.

March 12, 1949.

Dear Mr. Dolmetsch,

I will write a little recorder work for you. Kindly give full particulars of the concert, and the latest date you would like to have the work. Please remind me of the compass of the recorder for which you would like the work written.

Best wishes,

Yours sincerely,

Edmund Rubbra

Edmund Rubbra's letter to Carl Dolmetsch that resulted in the composition of
Meditazioni sopra 'Cœurs désolés'

Little can Carl have imagined from this letter that the resulting composition would become among his favourite and most frequently-played pieces. Indeed Edgar Hunt considered *Meditazioni* one of the finest works for recorder composed in the 20th century.

Rubbra's composing commitments in the early 1950s were such that he was not always able to fulfil Dolmetsch's requests for new works. This did not deter Carl who, in 1954, managed to secure the promise of another new piece from Rubbra, his *Fantasia on a Theme of Machaut* for recorder, string quartet and harpsichord. However, according to a letter from the composer written in November 1954, during the earliest stages of composition the piece was working out better with string trio. Dolmetsch responded immediately advising that a string quartet had already been engaged for the 1955 Wigmore Hall recital, so Rubbra duly completed the work, employing string quartet as initially requested. The result is impressively sonorous and it is perhaps fortuitous that circumstances resulted in the present scoring.

The *Meditazioni* is founded on a chanson by Josquin des Prés, and it was another des Prés chanson, 'Plusieurs regrets', on which Rubbra based his *Passacaglia*. In January 1962 he wrote to Dolmetsch., 'The "Passacaglia sopra Plusieurs regrets" is finished and I think it is my best yet. Hope you agree when you see it!' This may come as something of a surprise to those for whom the *Meditazioni* is a favourite. Correspondence after the first performance reveals Rubbra's concern at one critic's charge that the work was too short. Carl suggested a way in which it might be extended, but assured Rubbra, 'I do not find it at all too short, since in playing it I get a sense of completeness and fulfilment from the work just as it stands.' Publication of the *Passacaglia* followed in 1964 just as Rubbra had conceived it.

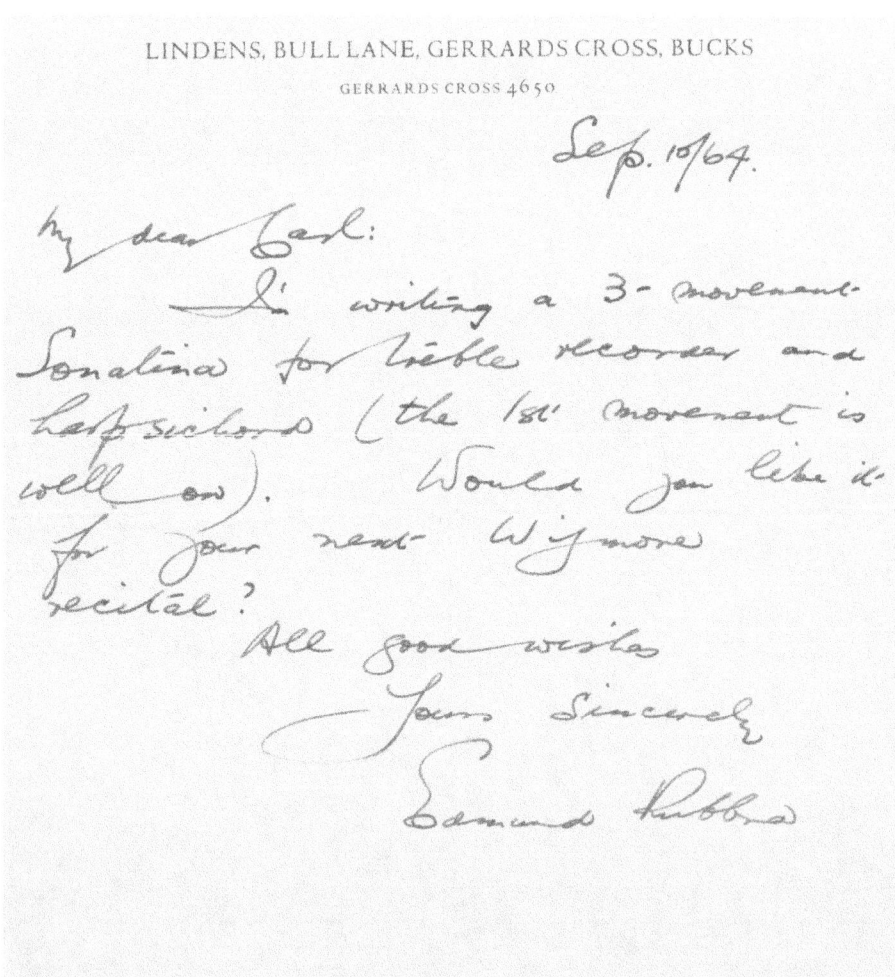

Edmund Rubbra's letter to Carl Dolmetsch announcing the composition of his Sonatina and offering it for performance at the next Wigmore Hall recital

Though, as previously noted, Rubbra had not always been able to respond immediately to Dolmetsch's requests for new works, in September 1964 the letter reproduced in facsimile above quite naturally created considerable enthusiasm and excitement! Rubbra's *Sonatina*, which received its premiere at the 1965 Wigmore Hall recital, is another masterpiece in the recorder's 20th repertoire.

It was to be 12 years before Dolmetsch approached Rubbra for another work, requesting a piece for recorder, violin, viola da gamba and harpsichord. Unfortunately Rubbra was busy fulfilling a number of commissions, but by chance one of these was from a composition pupil, Kenneth McLeish, for a work for recorder and harpsichord. Rubbra asked McLeish if he would be amenable to Dolmetsch premiering the work at his next Wigmore Hall recital. McLeish was delighted; the work, *Fantasia on a Chord*, was being composed to celebrate his and his wife Valerie's tenth wedding anniversary (as indicated by the dedication in the published edition).

Dolmetsch's daughter Marguerite, playing viola da gamba, was to take part in the recital, so Rubbra was requested if it would be possible to supply an optional part for the gamba doubling the harpsichord left hand. Rubbra supplied this (though the gamba does more than simply double the harpsichord, sometimes doubling the recorder an octave lower, and occasionally having entirely independent material). So *Fantasia on a Chord* acquired its present scoring and received its first performance at the Wigmore Hall on 9th March 1978. It is evident from correspondence regarding the gamba part that the repeat in the published edition was included at Dolmetsch's suggestion, and later correspondence between Rubbra and Dolmetsch, following the first performance, reveals that further revisions to the work were subsequently made. Though Rubbra had attended the first performance, on receiving a recording of the work from Dolmetsch he explained in a letter dated 13th September 1978;

> I am grateful to you for sending me the tape containing my new Fantasia, for, listening to it objectively, I have been able to pin-point an aspect of it that has been worrying me ever since the first performance. The material remains the same, for I am very happy about this, but I am re-shaping its rhythmic presentation. I am sure that, when you get the revised manuscript, you will feel that the increased suppleness has improved the piece enormously.

Comparison of the original and the final published versions enables the extent of Rubbra's revisions to be determined. The chord (A D E G# C# F), devised by Kenneth McLeish and which Rubbra noted consisted of 'an intriguing collection of varied intervals' on which the work is founded and its thematic material is also derived, remain intact. However, the original common-time time signature at the opening is changed to 3/2 and the note values halved.

After Rubbra's death in February 1986, Dolmetsch played the *Meditazioni* at his Wigmore Hall recital that year as a tribute to the composer whose friendship he cherished and from which had resulted some of the most significant works for recorder in the instrument's 20th-century repertoire.

In addition to Edmund Rubbra, another composer with whom Dolmetsch had a long and musically fruitful association was Gordon Jacob. Born in 1895, and for many years a very practical teacher of composition at the Royal College of Music in London (where he had himself been a pupil of Stanford and Howells) Jacob additionally acquired a reputation for his instrumental music, and particularly his skill in writing for wind instruments. It was probably as a result of this that Carl first approached him early in 1957 with a request for a new work for recorder. They arranged to meet at Jacob's home and, evidently keen to acquaint himself at first hand with the recorder, Jacob sent Dolmestch the short note on a postcard reproduced in facsimile below.

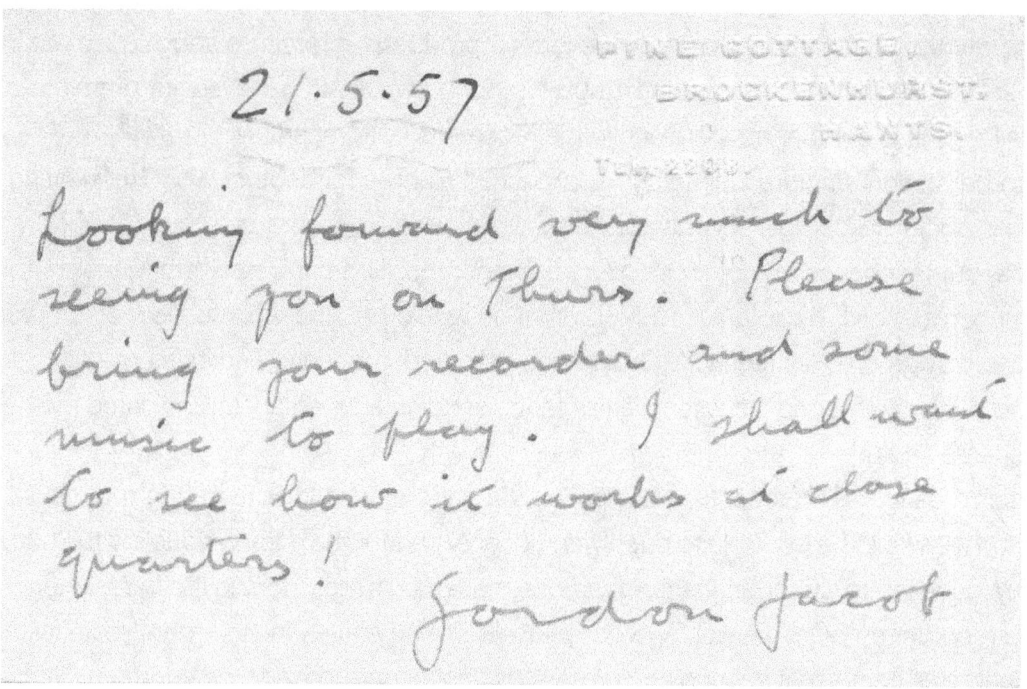

Postcard from Gordon Jacob to Carl Dolmetsch ahead of their meeting to discuss the composition of what was to become the Suite for recorder and string quartet (or small string orchestra)

The resulting work, the *Suite* for recorder and string quartet (or small string orchestra), shows just how rapidly and thoroughly Jacob acquired the ability to write entirely idiomatically for the recorder. From its premiere with the Martin String Quartet in Dolmetsch's 1958 Wigmore Hall recital, the *Suite* achieved critical acclaim. Jacob was delighted, but apparently surprised by the work's success, noting in a letter to Dolmetsch;

> I shall be most interested to hear how it goes with String. Orch. at Newcastle. Alan Frank [head of music publishing at Oxford University Press] is most enthusiastic about it and thinks it is one of my best works.'

Jacob's rather touching response to the success of the *Suite* is again evident in another letter to Dolmetsch following the performance in Newcastle with string orchestra in which Jacob wrote;

> I never imagined for a moment that this work would arouse enthusiasm like this. I think it must be your persuasive playing of it that is chiefly responsible, also perhaps that I treated the recorder as a perfectly normal musical instrument, which it is, and not in any way as a museum piece. Anyway, there it is!

Dolmetsch played the *Suite* on many subsequent occasions and, from its very much worn and repaired state, used Jacob's original manuscript recorder part long after the published edition had been produced by Oxford University Press.

Three further works by Jacob were premiered by Dolmetsch at the Wigmore Hall: *Variations* for recorder and harpsichord in 1963, *A Consort of Recorders* for recorder quartet (first London performance) in 1973, and *Trifles* for recorder, violin, cello and harpsichord (under the title *Suite*) in 1983.

Trifles was the last work Jacob composed for Dolmetsch – almost; in 1981, to mark Carl's 70th birthday, Jacob sent him *An unfinished 70-note tune for Carl's ...ieth birthday* (which is reproduced in facsimile in the section on birthday pieces), another token of their friendship that lasted until Jacob's death in 1984.

Other correspondence gives many insights into various aspects of the compositional process. We learn, for instance, that Dolmetsch's original request to York Bowen was for a work for recorder and harpsichord, but the composer instinctively wrote in an idiomatic way for the piano (he was a virtuoso pianist) and thus his *Sonatina* Op. 121 is scored for piano rather than harpsichord. Bowen himself took part in the Wigmore Hall premiere in May 1947.

In 1964 Carl requested Arnold Cooke for a work for recorder, violin, cello and harpsichord which could be premiered with the Schoenfeld sisters and Joseph Saxby at the 1965 Wigmore Hall recital. In a letter to Dolmetsch, written before starting work on composition, Cooke referred to the piece simply as *Quartet* for recorder, violin, cello and harpsichord, but on sending the completed score to Dolmetsch advised that he had decided to call it *Sonata*. This was because it related to the older type of sonata for various instruments with harpsichord from the baroque period, whilst the title quartet suggested rather more the type of chamber composition from the classical period. When the piece was submitted for publication the publishers wished to restore the original title of 'Quartet', as it reflected the work's scoring. Cooke preferred the stylistic description of the title 'Sonata', but ultimately the publisher was insistent, so the composer reluctantly had to concede.

From correspondence with Richard Arnell in connection with the work he composed for the 1966 Wigmore Hall recital we learn of what was perhaps the most unusual inspiration of any of the works composed for Dolmetsch. Arnell's *Quintet 'The Gambian'* for recorder and string quartet, following a dissonant and declamatory introduction, concludes with a set of variations on a tune written by his friend The Reverend John Faye, High Commissioner for the Gambia in London. As Arnell explained in a letter dated 26th November 1965, Faye had composed the tune two years earlier as an entry in a competition to choose a new national anthem for the Gambia to mark its independence. Arnell had helped him with the arrangement, but unfortunately it was placed only second. Its inclusion in this new work was a conciliatory tribute to the composer's friend.

It is indeed fortunate that Carl Dolmetsch retained so much of his correspondence, particularly that with composers, for it contains details of which we would otherwise know little or nothing in connection with the works composed for him, and which form a unique part of the history of the recorder's 20th-century revival.

Carl Dolmetsch: **A Centenary Celebration**

WORKS COMPOSED FOR CARL DOLMETSCH AND JOSEPH SAXBY

Carl and Joseph's extraordinary musical partnership that 'endured', as Greta Dolmetsch noted, for sixty years, was also, as she described it, 'the only one of its kind'. They first met in 1932 when both were engaged to provide music for an Oxford Playhouse production of Shakespeare's *Twelfth Night*, Carl playing recorder and Joseph the spinet. Carl immediately recognised Joseph's talent and invited him to take part in the Haslemere Festival; their musical collaboration continued from then on. They toured and performed together extensively, both in the UK and abroad, including the USA, Canada, Australia, New Zealand, Japan, South America and almost the whole of Europe.

Joseph and Carl at a rehearsal

Such was the nature of their combined artistry that a number of the new works they premiered at the Wigmore Hall were dedicated to them both. These include:

Edmund Rubbra	*Meditazioni sopra 'Cœurs désolés'*
Alan Hovhaness	*Sextet*
Gordon Jacob	*Variations*
John Gardner	*Little Suite in C*
Nigel Butterley	*The White-Throated Warbler*
Donald Swann	*Rhapsody from Within*

Of the above, Jacob's *Variations* and Swann's *Rhapsody from Within* were composed to celebrate the 30th and 50th anniversaries respectively of Carl and Joseph's musical partnership.

Three other works composed for and dedicated to them, but not premiered at the Wigmore Hall have also been published:

Christopher Wood	*Sonata di camera*
David Dorward	*Concert-Duo*
Michael Short	*Sonatina No.1*

Two further works composed for them have not previously been published, and we are pleased to be able to include them here.

The first is *Sonatina domestica* for descant recorder and harpsichord composed by Reginald Johnson in 1983; another piece to mark the 50th anniversary of the Dolmetsch/Saxby partnership. He was the schools music advisor for the county of Dorset and organised a rolling programme of recitals that, over a period of about 20 years, brought Carl and Joseph to every school in the area every three years. A particular party piece on occasions was his performance with Joseph of four hands at the harpsichord. He also made a number of arrangements of music for recorders and edited some of Gabrieli's music for Universal Edition. The cover of the manuscript score is inscribed:

For Carl and Joseph
for the
Fiftieth Anniversary of their Partnership

At the foot of the page is written:

> Carl – his copy
>   from
>   Reginald – his perpetration

Reginald Johnson's letter enclosing the work is also somewhat self effacing and reads as follows:
My dear Carl,

Having regard for the longstandingness (is there such a word?) of our association I felt I should like to do something beyond making a delightful visit to Town to honour the fifty years of collaboration between you and Joseph. For a long time I could not think what it should be: but in the end (although I know that I am not one of the World's Great Composers) I decided to follow the example of Robert Bridges and say
> "I, too, will something make
> And joy in the making."

And now it is done; and having been vetted by my (much) younger critics and passed as acceptable I send it to you with a Shakespearian envoi –
> "A poor thing, but mine own!"

I hope that it may be of some small use on occasion. Joseph will have his own copy – as he has his own plate!

        as ever,
        Reginald

The reference to "his own plate" is in connection with two specially commissioned plates made for Carl and Joseph by the German potter Mary Wandrausch to celebrate 50 years of their musical partnership.

Despite the composer's reservations it is a fun piece, and the following pages contain a facsimile of the manuscript score. We have also provided a computer set version of the score and a recorder part in the separate performing material. These include Carl's dynamic markings, originally indicated in a photocopy of the manuscript recorder part, which we have indicated in square brackets. Carl also added a trill and, in the last bar, an octave leap to the final note, which have been shown as an *ossia*. An editorial metronome mark has been added to supplement the original Allegro indication.

Works composed for Carl Dolmetsch and Joseph Saxby

Works composed for Carl Dolmetsch and Joseph Saxby

(WOODSTOCK)

Carl Dolmetsch: **A Centenary Celebration**

Works composed for Carl Dolmetsch and Joseph Saxby

The second work is Michael Short's *Giocata*, also for descant recorder and harpsichord. Details of the commission and a programme note are included on the title page of the manuscript score, reproduced in facsimile below.

GIOCATA

FOR DESCANT RECORDER & HARPSICHORD (OR PIANO)

BY

MICHAEL SHORT

COMMISSIONED BY WESTHAM ADULT RESIDENTIAL COLLEGE WITH ASSISTANCE FROM WEST MIDLANDS ARTS, TO MARK THE 40TH ANNUAL RECORDER COURSE PRESENTED THERE BY CARL DOLMETSCH & JOSEPH SAXBY.

PROGRAMME NOTE

If the word Sonata comes from 'suonare' (to sound), then Giocata (pronounced 'Joe Carter') can be derived from 'giocare' (to play – as in a game). By good fortune, the first two syllables are also those of the names Joseph and Carl, to whom the piece is dedicated. The music is playful throughout – motifs appear, are toyed with, disappear, and sometimes re-appear later – the whole in a light-hearted, improvisatory style.

MS.

The first page of the manuscript score is also provided in facsimile on the following page. Joseph Saxby's annotations are clearly visible. From Michael Short's very neatly written manuscript score and recorder part we have provided a computer set score and recorder part in the separate performing material.

Works composed for Carl Dolmetsch and Joseph Saxby

Carl Dolmetsch: **A Centenary Celebration**

A unique little piece, not written for Carl and Joseph but by Joseph for Carl, is *Improvisation* for treble recorder solo. It seemed appropriate to include it here. A facsimile of the manuscript is reproduced below and a computer set version is included in the separate performing material.

Perhaps its footnote provides a hint of the many discussions on performance that must have taken place between the two men, whose musical collaboration, even in 1951 when the piece was composed, was approaching twenty years.

Joseph died on 23rd June, and Carl on 11th July 1997 and it seems particularly poignant that there were just 17 days between – an important era in recorder history had come to an end.

Works composed for Carl Dolmetsch and Joseph Saxby

The two portraits below capture something of their relationship - the first was clearly a publicity shot; the second shows them in discussion at a rehearsal and reflects that taken many years earlier, and included on the first page of this section.

Carl Dolmetsch: **A Centenary Celebration**

BIRTHDAY PIECES COMPOSED FOR CARL DOLMETSCH

Among the various manuscripts in the archive are a number containing short pieces written by friends and colleagues to celebrate some of Carl's 'significant' birthdays. The shortest of these, however, is undated, so it is not possible to tell which birthday it celebrated. *Fuga à 3* is ascribed to 'Anon. Master of the C20', but a note in Carl Dolmetsch's handwriting below its single line of music identifies the composer as Walter Bergmann. It is reproduced in facsimile below.

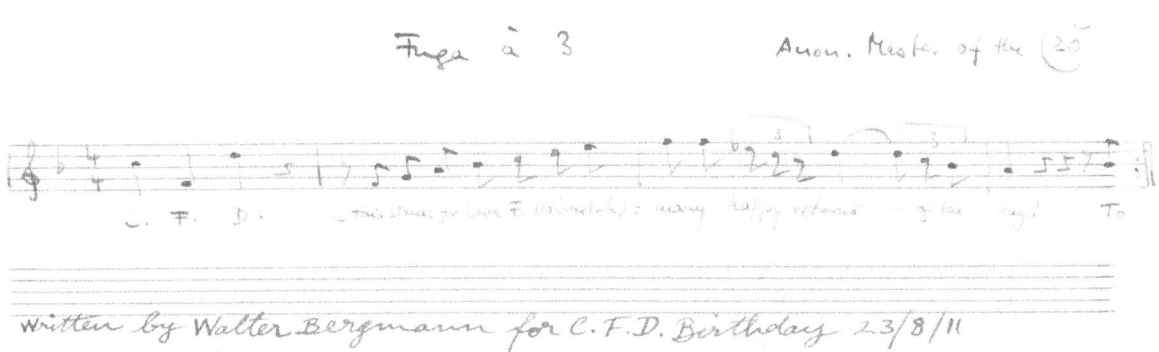

Beginning with the musical notes that represent Carl Dolmetsch's initials, this little piece is perhaps a perpetual canon rather than a fugue as such. Realizing the composer's intentions as to where the voices enter is quite straightforward and, once this is established, the number of ways in which it can be sung or played (or both) are many. In the performing material we have included a version with the original underlay that can be sung, with accompanying instruments if desired. In addition we have also included a version for recorders (its F major tonality fits comfortably on any size) or other instruments since, when not restricted by the text, it is possible to find a satisfactory place to conclude rather than letting the voices exit one by one as in the sung version.

For his 70th birthday Carl received a musical greeting from his old friend Gordon Jacob. *A 70-note Tune for Carl's ...ieth birthday* is written on a single sheet of the large-stave manuscript paper Jacob used during the later years of his life. Below this fragment scored for 'Recorder of any shape or size' Jacob wrote: 'With cordial greetings from Gordon, and best wishes for at least 30 more notes.' At the top right, in Carl's hand is written 'August 1981'.

Unfortunately, and we have counted very carefully a number of times, the piece contains only 69 notes. However, it is the sentiment and the occasion that count, and a facsimile of this charming musical greeting is reproduced below.

In the performing material we have included the original unfinished tune and provided our suggestions for completion. These take the total number of notes to one hundred in celebration of Carl Dolmetsch's centenary. You may also like to try your hand at the exercise!

Carl Dolmetsch: A Centenary Celebration

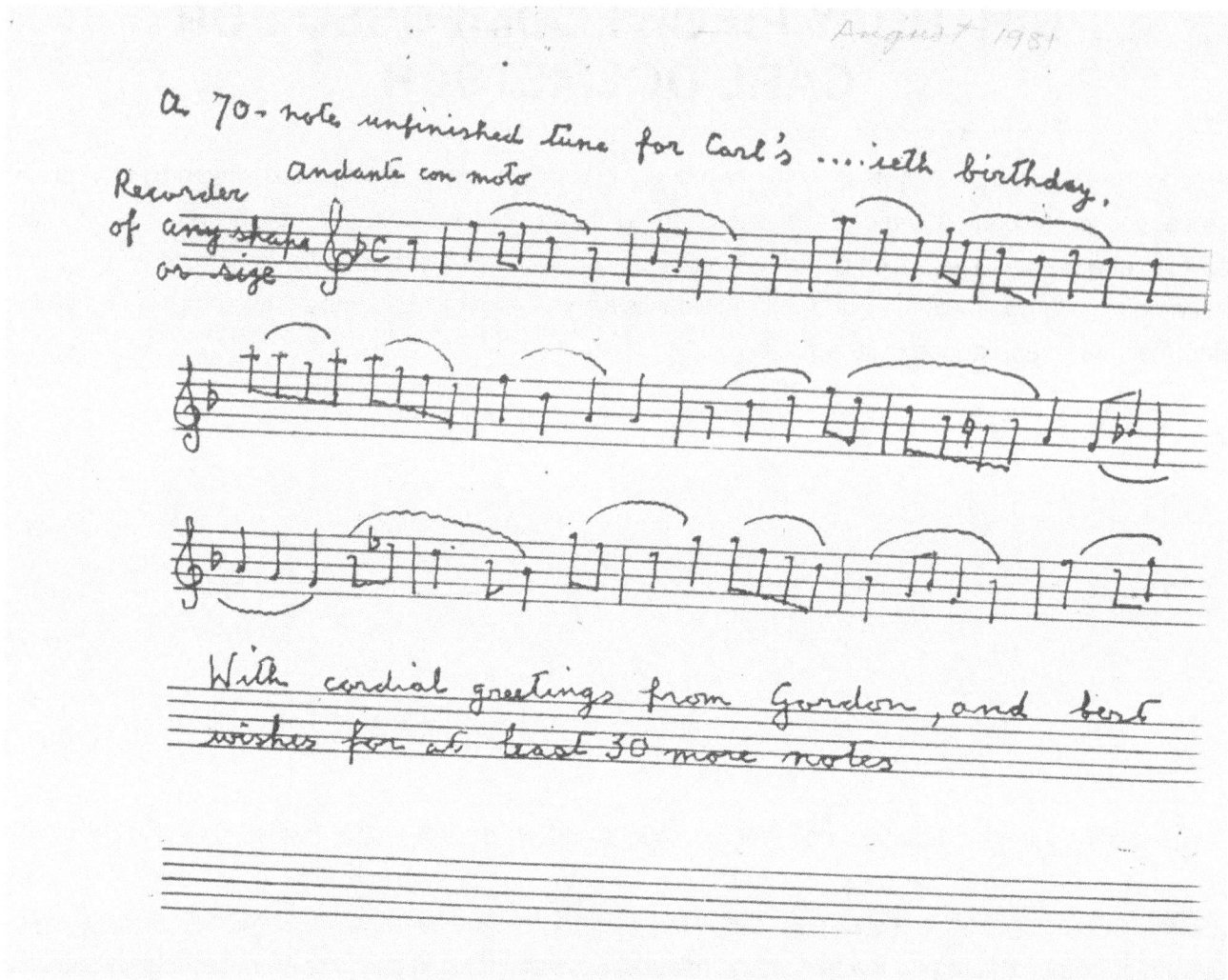

Gordon Jacob's '70-note unfinished birthday tune'

To mark his 80th birthday Carl received two celebratory pieces. That from Michael Short, *Les Quatre Vingts – fantaisie sur le nom 'C. D.'* for descant recorder solo, is another piece composed to contain the appropriate number of notes, but unlike Gordon Jacob's is complete; it also begins with the notes C D in representation of Carl's initials. As will be seen from the facsimile, it is written out so that each of its four lines contains twenty notes (the 'four twenties' of the title). Michael Short is a Dolmetsch family friend and was composer in residence at the Dolmetsch Summer School for a total of thirteen years. Among his compositions are a Sonatina for treble recorder and harpsichord (1979) for Carl Dolmetsch and Joseph Saxby (published by Studio Music), and his *Sinfonia* for treble recorder, string quartet and harpsichord was premiered at the 1985 Dolmetsch Wigmore Hall recital.

The other 80th birthday celebratory piece, William Godfree's *C. F. D. – A Birthday Present*, for descant recorder and piano, as in Walter Bergmann's *Fuga à 3*, presents Carl's initial letters as the notes of its theme. A facsimile of the manuscript is included below. William Godfree is an organist and another Dolmetsch family friend of many years.

In addition to the facsimiles we have included both the pieces in the performing material, that for *C. F. D. – A Birthday Present* as a score and separate recorder part. In the score we have, with the composer's permission, added some editorial indications for piano pedalling. He also requested that the final note in bar 18 of the recorder part be changed to a B-flat.

What better way to celebrate Carl Dolmetsch's centenary than to get together with friends and play these pieces, especially on 23rd August!

Birthday Pieces Composed for Carl Dolmetsch

Michael Short's 'Les Quatres Vingts'

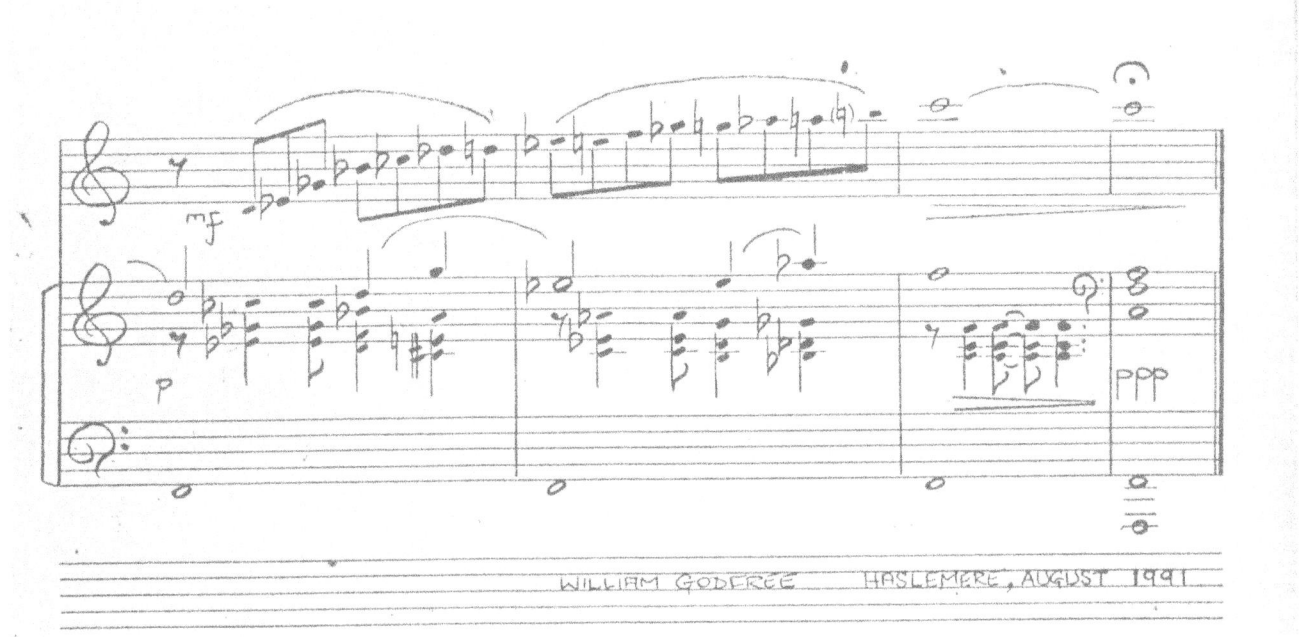

Willam Godfree's 'C. F. D. – A Birthday Present'

Mention should also be made of the piece Colin Hand composed in 1971 for Carl Dolmetsch's 60th birthday. *Sonata alla Cadenza* was a single-movement work falling into four clearly defined sections and making use of unaccompanied sopranino, descant, treble and tenor recorders. It was also monothematic, all its melodic material being derived from the opening theme founded on the intervals of the perfect fourth and the major seventh, together with its inversion, the minor second. The third section was the cadenza proper that gave the work its title. However, as Colin explained in a letter to Carl in December 1972, he was never entirely satisfied with a work for unaccompanied recorder. He therefore transposed the sections for sopranino, descant and tenor to be played on treble, and provided a piano accompaniment. Schott and Co. were interested in publishing it in its revised scoring, but had doubts about the long unaccompanied cadenza, which had been retained, in a work for treble recorder and piano. Colin reluctantly permitted the cadenza to be omitted, but noted that the original title would no longer be appropriate. No new title came immediately to mind, but he eventually suggested *Sonata Breve*. Under this title it was published by Schott in 1977 (edition 11265) and carries the original dedication:

To Carl Dolmetsch with affection,
on his 60th birthday: August 23rd 1971

The more concentrated form of the published version, achieved through the various revisions and the omission of the cadenza, enhances the monothematic structure and provides a more concise work that is well worth playing.

Carl Dolmetsch: **A Centenary Celebration**

A GAVOTTE FOR FOUR RECORDERS

In January 1928 Carl's elder brother Rudolph composed his *Air and Minuet* for recorder trio, descant, treble and tenor. It was published in 1992 by PRB Productions, Albany, California (in their Contemporary Consort Series No. 29). Just four month later in April 1928 Arnold Dolmetsch composed a three movement work, *Fantasie, Ayre and Jigg* for the same trio combination. It was published in 1948 as part of the series of original works for recorder instigated by the Society of Recorder Players in 1938 and printed by Schott and Company Limited. Though founded on early music idioms, these two pieces were among the earliest to be composed for recorder consort in its twentieth-century revival.

Carl knew both these trios. (He later recounted how he, together with his sisters Cecile and Natalie, played the *Fantasie, Ayre and Jigg* to their father towards the end of his life. Having listened to it Arnold commented 'I like that – what is it?'). Recorder consort music from the sixteenth century, particularly for quartet, was a prominent feature of Dolmetsch recital programmes, and in 1929, clearly influenced by this, Carl contributed a piece of his own to the twentieth-century recorder ensemble repertoire. His *Gavotte for Four Recorders* (descant, treble, tenor and bass) is reproduced here in facsimile, and a computer set version is included in the performing material.

In preparing this we have added editorially what is obviously a missing sharp to the last quaver f" in the first triplet group in the treble part at bar 8 without further comment. (This will also apply to the second quaver f" of the second triplet group in the same bar). On the presumption that it was probably an error, we have also omitted the sharp to the tenor's minim c" in bar 14, preferring to delay the cadence in the major until the final bar. The tempo indication 'Fast' has been supplemented by an editorial metronome mark of minim = 84.

It should be noted that the manuscript is in the hand of Carl's first wife, Mary, who also wrote out the manuscript score of Carl's *Theme and Variations* in A minor for descant recorder and harpsichord, of which he gave the premiere at his first recital in London's Wigmore Hall on 1st February 1939.

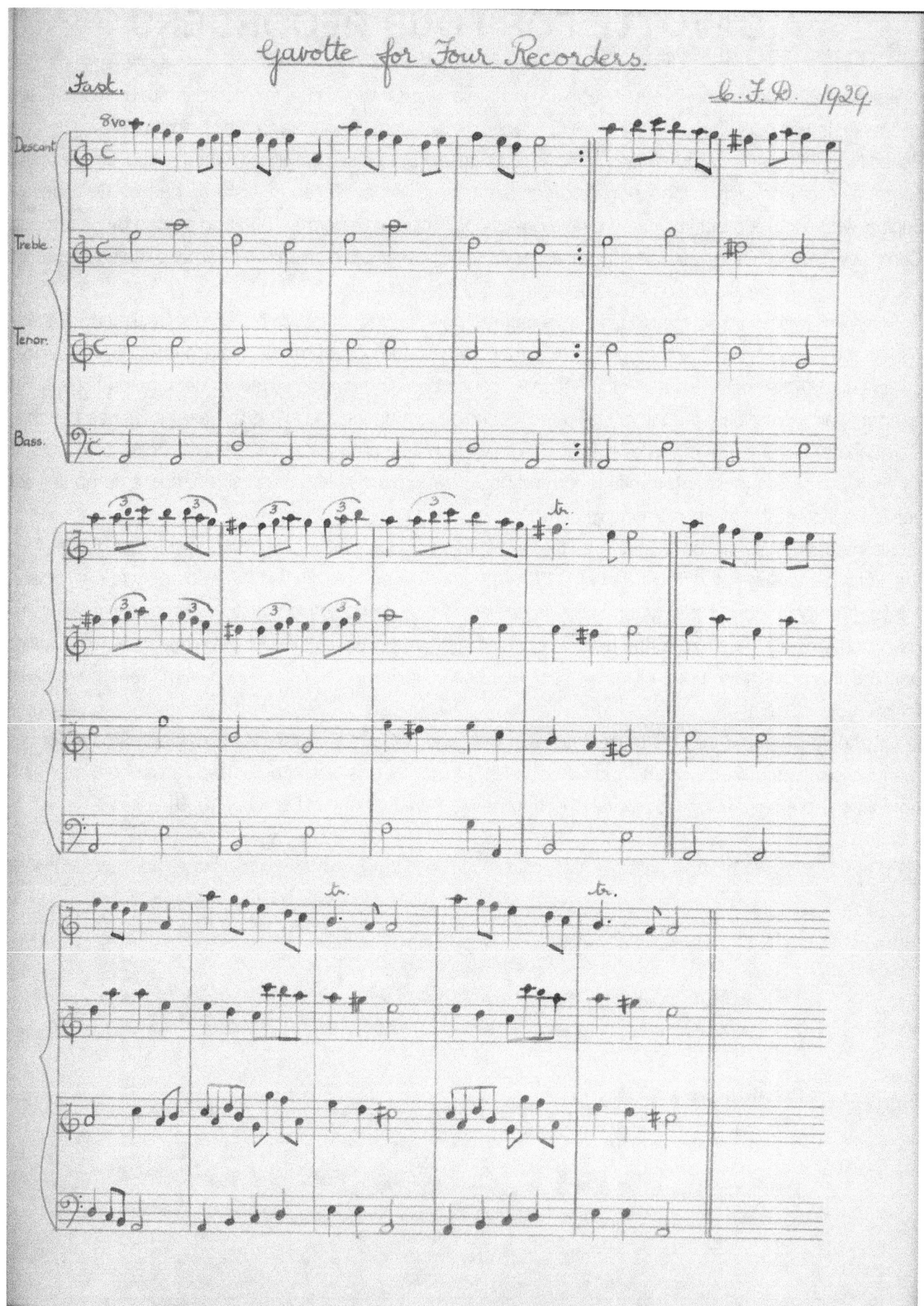

Manuscript of Carl Dolmetsch's Gavotte for Four Recorders

TWO PIECES FOR BASS RECORDER AND HARPSICHORD

Though the early and contemporary repertoire for treble recorder is extensive, that for the tenor, descant and sopranino is less so. For the bass, however, the repertoire has always been considerably more restricted, even during its revival. A manuscript score and recorder part in the archive of a piece entitled *Ayre (Gavota)* is headed 'Anon: set for Bass Recorder by: Carl Dolmetsch 3rd Sept: 1951'. Despite the anonymous attribution, as we shall see, this piece was composed by Carl himself and clearly intended to provide an original work for bass recorder, albeit in a baroque style. The manuscript score has pencil markings that introduce semiquaver figuration for the recorder, and these are indicated in a manuscript recorder part at the bottom of which is noted 'Revised November 2nd 1969, while in Vancouver, Canada'.

The inclusion of children's concerts as part of the Haslemere Festival enabled children from local schools (and indeed those further afield) to experience the world of early music in general and that of the recorder in particular. At these, Carl Dolmetsch liked to programme a series of pieces to demonstrate the various sizes of recorder, usually with harpsichord accompaniment. Although he had the *Ayre*, there was clearly the need for further bass recorder pieces, and the archive contains the manuscript of a similarly scored piece with the title *Borey*, though a later copy calls it 'Allegro (formerly Borey) in F'. Nevertheless, we have preferred the original title as being more indicative of its character. The heading in the manuscript score 'Haslemere Festival Children's Concerts 1966' clearly identifies its function and the date, but the indication 'anon. arr. Carl Dolmetsch 11th June' was very much tongue in cheek – as in the case of the *Ayre*, Carl was most certainly the composer! It will be noticed that the harpsichord part in the first and second halves is identical, and that the recorder part essentially, though not exactly, inverts the figuration of the first half in the second.

Its typical inclusion in such a sequence (under the title of *Allegro in F*, and with anonymous attribution) is shown in the programme for two children's concerts given during the Haslemere Festival in July 1986.

THE RECORDER FAMILY: PIECES FROM FOUR NATIONS

"Aria con divisioni"	(descant)	Nicola Matties c.1670
Largo in G minor	(tenor)	Henry Purcell 1659-1695
Allegro in F	(bass)	Anon English 17th century
Allegro in C	(treble)	G. P. Telemann 1681-1767
"Le Petit Rien"	(sopranino)	François Couperin 1668-1733
Tambourin	(piccolino)	Louis de Caix d'Hervelois 1670-1760

Incidentally, the piccolino recorder is a tiny instrument playing an octave higher than the descant which Dr Carl produced from his jacket breast pocket to play!

The success of the *Borey* prompted the composition of yet another piece for bass recorder and harpsichord, *Tempo di Gavotta*. The original manuscript does not include a date or the name of the composer, but a later photocopy is marked 'Anon. 18th century' above which 'C. F. D. 1978' is written in pencil. Despite another anonymous attribution there is no doubt of Carl's authorship; a manuscript part for cello (or gamba) is headed "Anon." English! – the inverted commas and exclamation mark are something of a giveaway.

Carl Dolmetsch: **A Centenary Celebration**

Carl Dolmetsch with bass recorder

In his last Wigmore Hall recital in October 1989 Carl Dolmetsch included an item headed 'Solo pieces for various recorders', much in the way he had done at children's concerts. As all but one of the works in the remainder of the programme were for treble recorder, this did not feature in the sequence. The pieces, which included the *Tempo di Gavotta* (with the composer's identity indicated), were as follows:

"Plaint"	(tenor)	Colin Hand
Variations on a theme by Herbert Howells	(descant)	Alan Ridout
"Tempo di Gavotta"	(bass)	Carl Dolmetsch
Air in the Lydian Mode from "Sequence"	(sopranino)	Alan Ridout

Two Pieces for Bass Recorder and Harpsichord

Inclusion of the *Tempo di Gavotta* was particularly appropriate, as in his first Wigmore Hall recital fifty years earlier Carl had premiered his *Theme and Variations in A minor* for descant recorder and harpsichord.

We have included facsimiles of the scores of the *Borey* and the *Tempo di Gavotta*, (though in reverse order to enable both halves of the *Borey* to be visible at the same time) and the score and a bass recorder part of each in the separate performing material. In the *Borey* we have followed the pencil indication in the manuscript score for the harpsichord part to be played *octava bassa*. This was evidently tried in rehearsal and is certainly effective. An editorial *rallentando* has been indicated at the close of the *Borey* to match that included in the manuscript of the *Tempo di Gavotta*. We have also rationalized the indications for repeats and the first and second time bars in both pieces.

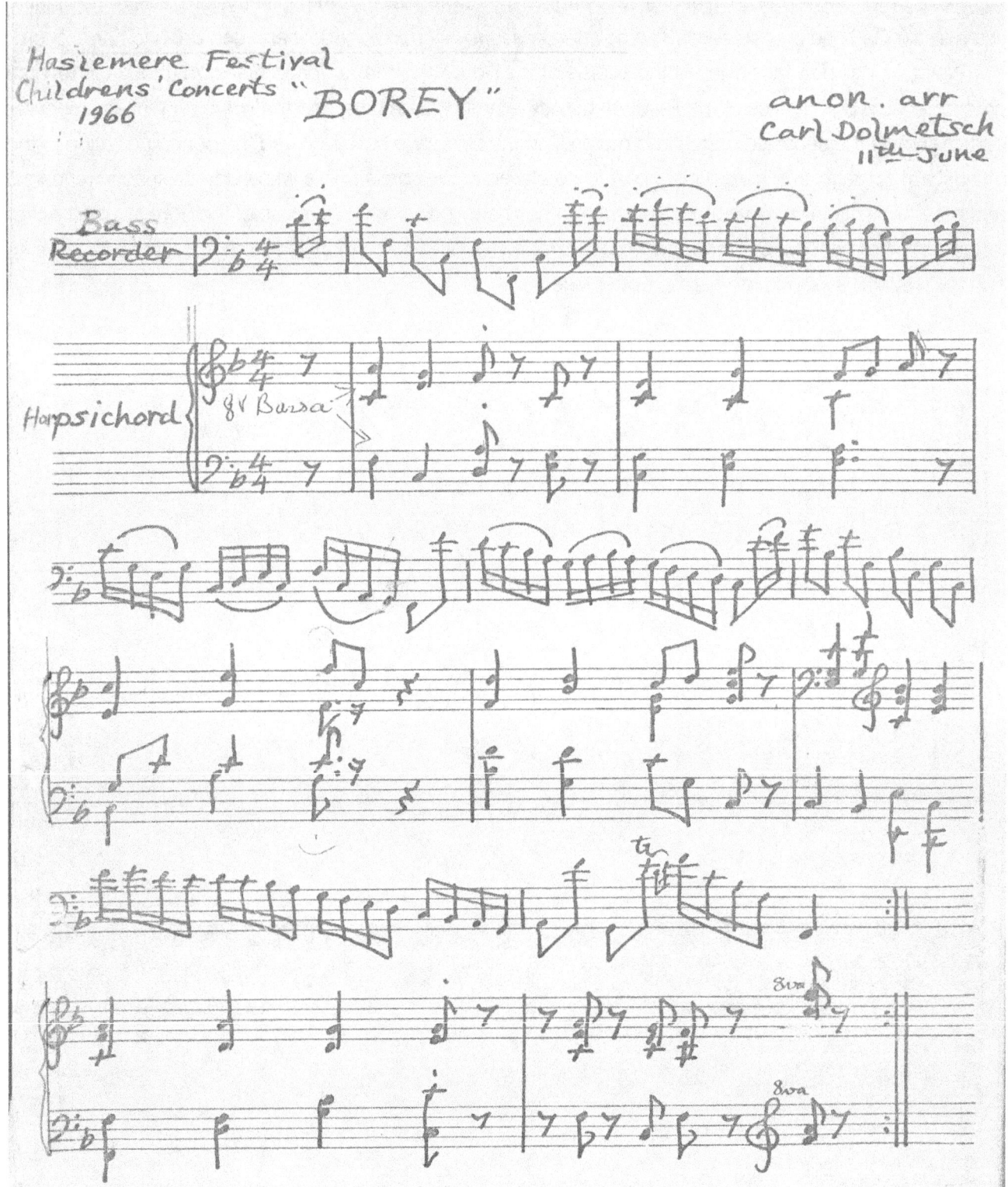

First page of the MS score of 'Borey'

Second page of the MS score of 'Borey'

The MS score of 'Tempo di Gavotta'

PIECES FOR TWO RECORDERS (ONE PLAYER)

In January 1933 Arnold Dolmetsch composed three little duets for two recorders (descant and treble). The manuscript (which is reproduced in facsimile in *A Birthday Album for the Society of Recorder Players* published by Forsyth Brothers, Manchester in 1987) is headed:

> 3 Duos pour 2 Recorders
> joués par une seule personne: (Carl!)

None has any tempo marking; the first is without title, the second is headed 'march' and the third simply 'duo'.

It is evident from these that Carl had mastered the technique of playing two recorders at the same time, and later composed some pieces of his own for performance in this way. Of course, not everyone can play two recorders at once, but the pieces can also be enjoyed by two players.

Carl playing two recorders

We have selected three of these pieces: the inventively titled *Fuguanon* dated 1966 (it begins in strict canon at the lower fifth, but includes a fugal type stretto entry of the subject and a tonic pedal point towards the end); *Siena Air* dated 1969 and *Pastorale en Rondeau* dated 1980, which in addition to the version for two unaccompanied recorders has an optional harpsichord part. All three are included both in facsimile and in the separate performing material. For the *Pastorale en Rondeau* we have provided a full score and a part for the two recorders. As the version with harpsichord includes an introduction and an interlude for the harpsichord alone, necessitating rests for the recorders, a separate part for the two recorders for the unaccompanied version has also been included. Inspection of the facsimiles of the manuscripts will reveal a chromatic *ossia* in quavers below bar 32 of *Fuguanon* which we have not reproduced in the performing material, and below *Siena Air*, a rather chromatic, short untitled sketch, for which we have also not provided a performing version. In the score of *Pastorale en Rondeau* a few of Joseph Saxby's annotations can be seen.

We have made a number of editorial amendments and additions in the printed performing material as follows:

Fuguanon   bar 16, descant part; quaver c replaced by crotchet, and quaver b-flat omitted.
bar 18, treble part; quaver f replaced by crotchet, and quaver e-flat omitted.
bars 32-32, treble part; semibreve d in bar 31 tied to crotchet d in bar 32.

Pastorale en Rondeau
Indications for repeats in refrain to be played *p*
Though the final statement of the refrain is marked 'senza rep' we felt that repeating it brought the piece to a more satisfactory conclusion. (The traditional Rondeau form is usually AABACAA)
Ritardandos indicated at the close of 1er and 2e couplets and final repeat of refrain.
bar 19, harpsichord right hand; final chord amended.
bar 28, harpsichord right hand, first chord amended for 1st time.

Pieces for Two Recorders (ONE player)

The MS of 'Fuguanon'

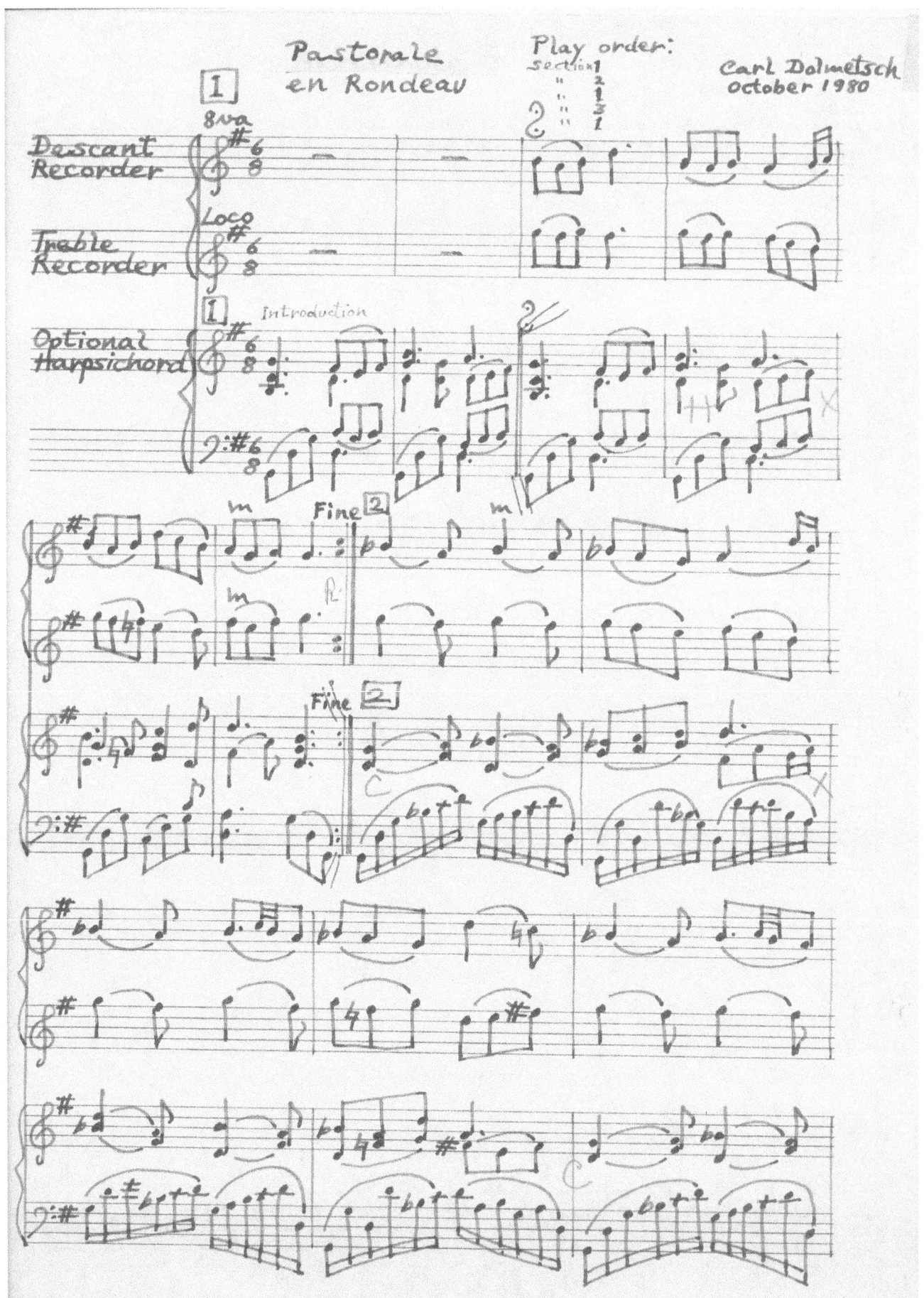

First page of the MS score of 'Pastorale en Rondeau'

Pieces for Two Recorders (ONE player)

Second page of the MS score of 'Pastorale en Rondeau'

The MS of 'Siena Air'

STUDIES TO IMPROVE RECORDER TECHNIQUE

Improving and maintaining recorder technique is a fundamental and essential part of any player's practice regime, and important to this is the use of studies, particularly those that concentrate on a particular aspect of technique.

Carl Dolmetsch's *Advanced Recorder Technique* (the third part of his recorder tutor first published by E. J. Arnold & Son of Leeds in 1954) included three studies based on early dance tunes for treble recorder, and a chromatic study arranged by Carl for descant recorder from Federico Fiorillo's *Caprice No. 19*.

It is intriguing to note that Carl even devised an individual study to assist in obtaining the fluency required in a problematic passage of Arnold Cooke's *Divertimento* for recorder and string quartet (first performed at the Wigmore Hall in 1960). It is un-barred and written out at the foot of the first page of the final movement in the manuscript recorder part, where it appears as follows:

It was clearly intended to assist with a passage that occurs at bars 16 to 20 and again at 33 to 37 which is as follows:

He was also at pains to ensure that his children had the means to acquire a fluent technique, and in 1966 composed a whole-tone study which, at the head of the manuscript is dedicated 'To Jeanne and Guite'. Though there is a chromatic study for descant recorder in *Advanced Recorder Technique* which could no doubt be transposed for treble, Jeanne felt that a chromatic companion for the original whole-tone study was required. Carl duly obliged, and the manuscript of the resulting study 'For Jeanne' dated 1992, is also in the archive. The date at the foot of the manuscript, it should be noted, is 25th December – Greta commented that Carl found writing out music very relaxing and enjoyable; this evidently extended to Christmas Day!

Facsimiles of both are reproduced here, and included in computer set form in the performing material, for which Jeanne has suggested suitable metronome marks. Nevertheless, as advised in connection with the studies in *Advanced Recorder Technique* 'Practice slowly at first and increase the speed by degrees. Begin with single tonguing and progress to double tonguing as you increase the tempo.'

First page of the MS of 'Chromatic Study'

Second page of the MS of 'Chromatic Study'

Carl Dolmetsch: A Centenary Celebration

The MS of 'Whole-tone Study'

www.ingramcontent.com/pod-product-compliance
Lightning Source LLC
Chambersburg PA
CBHW081436300426
44108CB00016BA/2381